MW01616862

Tracey K. Hurst & Patricia E. Uribe

All rights reserved. No part of this publication may be reproduced, distributed, or transmitted in any form or by any means, including photocopying, recording, or other electronic or mechanical methods, without the prior written permission of the authors, except in the case of brief quotations embodied in critical reviews and certain other noncommercial uses permitted by copyright law. For permission requests, write to the author at echsguidebook@gmail.com with, "Attention: Permissions," in the subject line.

Copyright © 2016 Hurst Educational Services for
Tracey K. Hurst & Patricia E. Uribe

All rights reserved.

ISBN: 0692661425

ISBN-13: 978-0692661420 (Hurst Educational Services)

Accelerated Success!

ECHS Structures & Systems

Book 3 from <u>Early College High School: An Intentional Design</u>

How your district can implement and sustain the best small school model for underserved populations

By Tracey K. Hurst and Patricia E. Uribe

Copyright © 2016 by Tracey K. Hurst and Patricia E. Uribe

Tracey K. Hurst & Patricia E. Uribe

PREFACE

It is our pleasure to provide this book as the final part of what is our 3-part series on the Early College High School design based on our combined fourteen years of experience working throughout Texas. The series is intended to help existing schools continually revisit the model with the goal of following it to fidelity, guide new schools with purposeful questions and sound information, and pique the interest of administrators thinking of beginning the ECHS journey. We are delighted to have completed the full manuscript, <u>Early College High School: An Intentional Design</u>, and look forward to future publication of the complete work in hard copy. We truly believe that the ECHS design provides a solution to society's valid questions around poor high school graduation rates, low college completion rates, and most recently, the $1.3 trillion debt incurred by US students through college loans.

If you take away only one message let it be this - ***the success of Early College High Schools is by design***. It is not luck; not a chance occurrence; nor is it simply because it is a small school. It works because dedicated professionals follow the design and work in partnership with colleges to create a positive secondary <u>and</u> higher education experience for our children. And it works because every person involved – the principal, the college liaison, the staff, and the students – believe in continuous improvement and strive to get better every day, **and** they all work hard every day.

We dedicate this work to our family and friends who have stood by our side on this journey. Putting our ideas, experiences, and knowledge into a comprehensive work was challenging, and as you can imagine, rewarding. We appreciate the continuous support and understanding as we spent endless hours to make this book a reality.

It is our hope that teachers, parents, and other school professionals will take away a comprehensive understanding of how and why the design works, and how schools across the country are using instructional elements from this design in their traditional schools.

For those reading that are new to ECHS and want to learn more, we feel confident that the knowledge conveyed in this book can help you establish the best early college high school in the country. Please visit www.echsguidebook.com for updates and additional information about workshops and upcoming titles.

Special thanks the people who enriched our knowledge of the content and process:

Yvette Cavazos, founding principal of Achieve ECHS (McAllen Independent School District)

Abigail Ruth Garza, Texas A & M International University

Scott Groen, teacher at Aldine Early College High School, Houston, TX

Kristinia Haney, teacher at Grapevine Colleyville Collegiate at Tarrant County NE Campus

Lauren Hobbs, teacher and instructional coach, Sheldon ECHS, Houston, TX

Jami Ivey, founding principal of Murchison Pinnacle ECHS (Athens Independent School District)

Bobbe Knutz, founding principal of Grapevine Colleyville Collegiate at Tarrant County Northeast Campus (Grapevine Colleyville Independent School District)

Janice Lombardi, principal of Trinidad Garza ECHS (Dallas Independent School District) since 2009

Rosie Olivera, principal of ECHS at Brookhaven from 2009 - 2013

Allen Painter, founding principal of Sheldon ECHS (Sheldon Independent School District

Usamah Rodgers, founding principal of Cedar Hill Collegiate (Cedar Hill Independent School District)

AUTHORS

Tracey K. Hurst

For the past decade, Mrs. Hurst has worked as an educational consultant, specializing in active engagement in the classroom including strategies, coaching, and assessment. She has visited 41 early college high schools across Texas, providing workshops and leadership & instructional coaching. Additionally, she works with traditional schools scaling the ECHS model elements K – 12 and those striving to incorporate student-centered learning activities in every class.

Mrs. Hurst previously served as Secondary Advanced Academics Director in Richardson Independent School District where her primary responsibilities were around the College Board programs and dual credit. She taught secondary mathematics, grades 7 - 12, as well as PreAP Geography -- a subject she is passionate about -- primarily at Lake Highlands High School. During a hiatus from education, she worked as the director of a non-profit affiliated with the Smithsonian Institution.

Mrs. Hurst holds a Bachelor of Arts Degree in Urban Planning from Binghamton University in New York and a Master's Degree in Curriculum and Instruction from George Mason University in Fairfax, Virginia.

Dr. Patricia E. Uribe

Dr. Uribe is the Director of the Texas Academy of International and STEM Studies and the Superintendent of Texas A&M International University Independent School District in Laredo, Texas. She is a published author and also serves as an Assistant Professor for the Department of Professional Programs, College of Education, Texas A&M International University.

Dr. Uribe has over twenty-five years of experience in public education and served as the founding principal for the Laredo/TAMIU Early College High School. In addition, Dr. Uribe is also an educational consultant and has served as a Leadership facilitator and External Instructional Coach for twenty-four Early College High Schools in south Texas.

Dr. Uribe holds a Bachelor of Science Degree in Political Science with a concentration in Legal Studies from Southwest Texas State University (Texas State University), a Master's Degree in Elementary Education and a Master's Degree in Educational Administration from Laredo State University (Texas A&M International University), and a Doctorate Degree in Educational Leadership from Texas A & M University Corpus Christi and Texas A & M University Kingsville. (Collaborative Program).

Other Works

Book 1 – ECHS Partnership and the MOU

ECHS Partnership and the MOU (Memorandum of Understanding) will help administrators understand the benefit of the ECHS design and how to implement it, including key questions for both partners. planning year decisions, budgets, and facilities. Like subsequent titles, the work is based on the principles of the model used nationwide.

KINDLE EDITION   HARD COPY EDITION

<table>
<tr><td><u>Book 1</u>   Partnerships & The MOU</td></tr>
<tr><td>Chapter 1—The Early College High School Concept</td></tr>
<tr><td>Chapter 2—Mission and Core Principles</td></tr>
<tr><td>Chapter 3—Pre-Planning Year Decisions</td></tr>
<tr><td>Chapter 4—The Partnership</td></tr>
<tr><td>Chapter 5—Memorandum of Understanding</td></tr>
<tr><td>Chapter 6—Budgets and Funding</td></tr>
<tr><td>Chapter 7—Facilities</td></tr>
<tr><td>Appendices include sample and actual MOUs, commentary on policy, reflective questions for new and existing ECHSs, and scenarios for discussion.</td></tr>
</table>

Book 2 – Students, Staff, & Other Stakeholders

The second book in the series focuses on the people involved with Early Colleges. From the target population, students traditionally underrepresented in higher education, to the staff, parents, and community – learn more about the unique nature of how early college impacts each group and vice versa.

KINDLE EDITION   HARD COPY EDITION

Tracey K. Hurst and Patricia E. Uribe

Book 3 – Academic Structures & Systems

Table of Contents

Chapter 1 - Early College High School Overview

Success Story

The turn of the century saw the emergence of arguably the best small school model to serve all adolescents: the Early College High School (ECHS). As compared to traditional high schools, this model has experienced significantly higher high school graduation rates, higher daily attendance rates, and a higher percentage of students earning college credit while in high school, with one in three ECHS students earning an associate's degree before their scheduled high school graduation (Webb, 2014). This is particularly remarkable because the target population of the ECHS is specifically those who have been historically underrepresented in higher education. American Institutes for Research (AIR), a third party in no way affiliated with any Early College High School or the groups spearheading the initiative, reported the positive impacts of the early college design providing telling statistics in their 2009 report. For example, low-income ECHS students are 8.5 times more likely to earn a college degree than their low-income comparison group (22.1 percent to 2.6 percent). Among minority students, the impact was even greater with an ECHS student being ten times more likely to earn a college degree (29.4 percent for ECHS students as compared to 3.0 percent for traditional students) when evaluated with a comparison group (Berger, 2014).

None of these outcomes, or the many other positive results in the research studies, comprehensive reports, and testimonials offered by individual early college high schools occurred by accident. Instead a purposeful design based on research and experience has been implemented by districts and charter schools willing to invest in the process.

ECHS Design

The design of the Early College High School is intentional and research based. It is a purposeful small school serving **500 or fewer students** which allows every staff member to know every student on some level, and requires a small enough faculty that professional collaboration and camaraderie both naturally occur and intentionally develop. The **100-125 student cohort** works well for the development of individual class sections (with 20-25 students in each class, 4 - 5 sections of each course are typically offered and each teacher teaches 5-6 classes).

Locating the ECHS either **on the college campus** or in close proximity establishes the building blocks for a culture of learning, highlighted by aligned curriculum from secondary school through the first two years of college. The design calls for open communication beyond the natural partnership needs. Unlike most traditional high schools, the ECHS design calls for **teachers and college instructors to sit side-by-side in professional development** sharing instructional practices as well as curricular demands.

The introduction of college classes at the freshmen level in high school is intentional as well. The high standards are able to be met by otherwise struggling 14 and 15 year olds because, again, by design, **scaffolds are in place to support student learning**. For example, most ECHSs have a freshmen level support class where note taking, study skills, use of a calendar, and participation in study groups are all learned and refined. Many colleges offer this class through their psychology departments and it is often the first opportunity for ECHS freshmen to earn college credit. Other ECHSs offer it within their own program of studies. Some schools use existing programs like AVID (Advancement Via Individual Determination, a nationwide program serving the same target audience as Early Colleges), while other districts develop their own curriculum for the class based on their students' needs and state standards. Note: there are some ECHSs that intentionally keep freshmen out of college classes during the first semester, working diligently to develop the habits of mind necessary for success.

Jobs for the Future's delineated best practices for Early College High School

- Integrating postsecondary approaches tailored to each early college school to create "college for all" culture.

- Strengthening partnerships with postsecondary institutions and state agencies by collaboratively tackling institutional barriers early college students may face.

- Utilizing creative budget repurposing for long-term sustainability of Early College Designs—a robust pattern across existing early college schools.

- Testing existing programs and gathering data longitudinally to determine which programs to model after and bring to scale.

Source: Webb, Michael, and Carol Gerwin. "Early college expansion: Propelling students to postsecondary success, at a school near you."

The ECHS design also finds the best schools characterized by a staff who continually strives for instructional coherence. Research done by Newmann (2011) et al, finds that schools that achieve the components of instructional coherence, including common language and the intentional analysis of *every* potential program under the lens of the benefits to instruction and learning, are the foundation for the development of college-ready students. In the authors' combined experiences, this might be the one defining characteristic that sets the good early colleges apart from the **great** early colleges. The work around vertical alignment also falls into these goals of coherence, and is instrumental in accelerating the preparation for college, a necessary component for individual student success.

Another part of the ECHS design is intentional school-wide structures whereby staff can observe, learn from, and provide feedback on instruction and learning from for one another. This occurs during common professional development time as well as during rounds - a system whereby educators visit one another's rooms. When organized and efficiently facilitated, the process can accelerate the professional development among all members of the staff. Comparable to rounds, *Looking at Student Work* protocols provide a structured examination of the student products, and when teachers utilize the provided protocols, they see how instruction can improve for all students. To learn more, visit lasw.org.

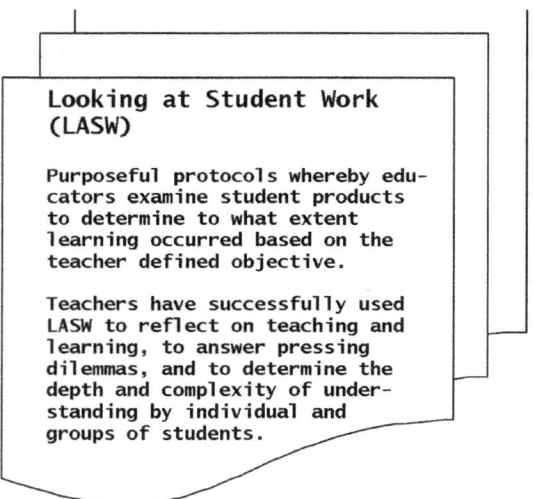

Looking at Student Work (LASW)

Purposeful protocols whereby educators examine student products to determine to what extent learning occurred based on the teacher defined objective.

Teachers have successfully used LASW to reflect on teaching and learning, to answer pressing dilemmas, and to determine the depth and complexity of understanding by individual and groups of students.

Throughout this volume, you will learn more about the purposeful academic structures and systems used by schools, principals, counselors, college instructors, and other staff, all working in unison to facilitate student learning. The rigorous standards, when upheld by all, result in a high percentage of high school graduates earning their associate's degrees, as well as the remaining students with up to 1.5 years of college credit - all at no expense to the student or family. While volume one focused on Partnerships and the MOU and volume two, Students, Staff, and Other Stakeholders, the material that follows truly focuses on school wide structures and classroom systems that support learning for all students. Intended to educate all stakeholders, teachers and administrators will find it especially valuable for their own professional development. There may be a few cases of content overlap among volumes; please know that it is intentional because the information is valuable and communicated under different lenses.

Chapter 2 - The Structure of ECHS Academics

The components that are markedly different from the structure of academics at a traditional high school revolve around the fact that, in order to be successful, students must be college ready at age 16 when they begin their junior year in high school and are now full-time college students. This occurs when a student is following the delineated plan for an associate's degree, and as the ECHS matures, typically 50-75% of students will be on this track. For example, reminding English teachers that they only have two years to teach the four years typically covered in high school English courses really hits home. The other key difference is the workload of the individual students. When the ECHS enrolls the freshmen into the 'typical' courses that a high school 9th grader takes (math, science, social studies, English, foreign language and one more elective) AND enrolls him into 2-3 one semester college classes, the workload is often too heavy. Instead, keeping the traditional schedule to only the four core and one elective *and one college class* is a better structure for success.

Typical Schedule for ECHS student in his 2nd year

Student: John Smith   Grade: 10

Fall Semester Schedule
MWF   **T Th**
HS English 3   HS Chemistry
HS Algebra 2   HS US History
HS MAPS (support class)   HS Health (1 sem)
College Speech   College US Gov't

Spring Semester Schedule
MWF   **T Th**
HS English 3   HS Chemistry
HS Algebra 2   HS US History
HS MAPS (support class)   HS Phys Ed
College Art History   College Spanish 2*

*inc lab component; also, students typically 'test' into the appropriate level of Spanish. Colleges have placement exams for most language courses. So starting college in Spanish 2 is not uncommon.

Credits that will be earned:
8.0 high school credits at 1.0 each for full year courses
12.0 college credits (3.0 in Speech, 3.0 US Gov't, 3.0 in Art History, 3.0 in Fundamentals of Spanish I)

This schedule is academically more rigorous than the typical high school sophomore with five high school academic classes and four additional college dual credit courses that have high standards, fewer interventions by the instructor, and fewer assessments to comprise the grade for the course.

Crosswalk

The core academic crosswalk or course sequence is designed to prepare all students for entry into a state's public four year university system and also provide the students with the opportunity to earn significant college credits while in high school. It is basically a side-by-side list of high school courses and college courses that will first and foremost, lead to a high school diploma and, at the same time, provide the opportunity to also earn an associate's degree. Meeting the basic requirements of both institutions is the key to success. Though some students will pursue bachelor's degrees at out of state and/or private universities, the ECHS typically aligns their crosswalk to their specific state college recognized coursework. This is based on the idea that a large percentage of ECHS graduates will be attracted to their own state university system both due to financial reasons as well as proximity to home.

The development of the crosswalk is an important activity, but not as daunting as one might initially think. The framework of the high school curriculum serves as the starting point, and alignment to the college courses, which in essence cover the same material but to a more rigorous standard and with more responsibility on the students, provides an accelerated path to potentially multiple college degrees. Remember, typically students who choose the ECHS route are giving up some of the specialty courses obtained with the flexibility of a high school schedule whereby electives allow the pursuit of multiple years of fine arts, athletics, or even greater depth in a core area. When planning the high school course sequence in an ECHS, there are simply fewer variables.

Institutions of higher education (IHEs) in many states have a standard or core set of academic courses that are transferable to any state institution of higher education (not to be confused with the widely accepted K-12 Common Core Standards which are used in public school curriculum in 47 states). For example, in North Carolina, there are a number of courses that are recognized statewide as part of the 44 credit hours that transfer to any North Carolina state college. The complete listing of courses that can comprise the specific requirements for North Carolina, nicely correlated to multiple associate's degrees, is available athttp://www.nccommunitycolleges.edu. Most campuses have the transferable courses listed on a PDF on their web site. For example, UNC - Chapel Hill, like the other North Carolina colleges and universities, states that, "Students who have completed the specified 44 hour requirement of the core curriculum in the NC Community College System will, upon admission, meet the freshman/sophomore general education requirements for Carolina's general liberal arts degrees with the exception of experiential education, global issues, lifetime fitness, and foreign language." Read more about UNC on the document they produced and available at http://tinyurl.com/zkx3ll2. [note: the last 4 characters are 3 – lower case L – lower case L – 2] Another example is available through North Carolina Central University's web site. Their document is available at http://tinyurl.com/zwqa7ny.

In Texas, there is a core 42 credit hours that are transferable to any state college in Texas. The Texas Higher Education Coordinating Board (THECB) has an excellent web page to examine the structure at http://statecore.its.txstate.edu/. California has a recognized degree plan designed to transfer to the four-year California State College system, and even designates these associate's degrees as *transfer* degrees. Learn more at http://tinyurl.com/zufm82m.

These three states exemplify what most states are doing to provide structure for students who choose the 2-year college route. By standardizing the requirements for all state schools, time and money are not wasted in coursework that will not transfer. Thus, we recommend that the ECHS develop their crosswalk from these recognized courses and their corresponding credits.

An excellent idea, in service to your students, is to ensure that all of your ECHS staff is well versed in the college requirements. This is not to say that they take the place of the counselor. Instead, it is to support the work of the counselor. The level of understanding does not need to be such that every teacher can serve as the counselor, but instead, the teachers should be able to answer students' basic questions, and when needed, direct the students to the correct resource (ECHS counselor, college counselor, specific web page, student handbook, etc.) Think about the 16-year old student that earns good grades, but is timid and reluctant to 'bother' the counselor. Most likely she will be willing to express her confusion or lack of understanding to one trusted teacher. Isn't it preferable to have that teacher be versed in the basics, thus valuing the process and the student's questions?

Articulation Agreements

It is important that curriculum leaders, such as the provost or university deans and their public school curriculum and instruction counterparts, meet to outline courses that will fulfill the high school requirements as well at the core curriculum <u>and</u> associate's degree for the university or college. An articulation agreement is often already in place for dual credit - <u>but Early College High School is different</u>. The number of courses in the existing articulation agreement will often not provide enough coursework to obtain the associate's degree. Remember, the dual credit agreement was designed for the higher achieving students and used to provide concurrent credit during the senior year. It is highly recommended that you create a new agreement where curriculum leaders outline requirements for each grade level of the ECHS years.

> An Articulation Agreement for Early College High Schools is an approved agreement between two institutions, the high school or charter <u>and</u> the Institute of Higher Education, which allows a student to apply credits earned in specific classes for graduation at one institution for transfer to graduation requirements at the other institution.

These articulated requirements will guide decisions on the best way for the school to provide opportunities to all students. For example, if the high school requirement includes four credits in the four core subjects (mathematics, social studies, English, and science), and the college requires six college credits in each of those areas, the listing begins. Six credits are typically earned in two semesters, and thus one year of high school course work. Determining where the college courses fit in to the sequence is part of the planning. It is not like the dual credit agreement whereby the motivated student or counselor ensures that the student who loves literature is taking the college British Literature course during the school year and two more literature classes in the summer. Instead, it is a purposeful blueprint that lays out the expectation for all students to follow, and then allows for contingencies when students struggle or are unable to complete the college degree plan for whatever reason (they must complete the high school plan).

It is worth stating here that throughout all of these books, there is no recommendation to ever support sending an ECHS student back to traditional school. When you choose to open an Early College High School, you are committing to serving a group of students who might not otherwise have a pathway to college, and truly, who might not have been previously served at times through their K-8 experience. **This will be difficult** - there is no question about it. While indeed a school of choice, ECHSs are not magnet schools. We truly believe in the fidelity of the model and have unfortunately seen repeated actions by ECHS principals to send students away because of immature behavior, the inability to be successful in ECHS high school courses, or other issues that would be faced in any traditional high school. This should not be an option – the ECHS staff must understand that when students enroll in the ECHS, they are there for their high school years.

Early college high school is a high school. Once students enroll, the expectation of everyone on staff needs to be that the student will be with them for four years. There is no better place to send a student who is underperforming, unappreciative of the opportunity before him/her, not able to satisfy the college entrance exam requirements, or any other reason. 99.5% of the students need to stay with you unless you can state, unequivocally, that he/she would be better off in the traditional high school.

1. Can the other school change the behaviors that are exhibited and frustrating?
2. Can the other school provide a better academic support system?
3. What exactly is offered at the other school to better support this child?

ECHS teachers and staff—teaching at an early college is difficult, challenging, and rewarding. Setting up the structures and systems is the key to helping all students achieve success.

We strongly recommend that you sincerely consider if it is truly in the best interest of the child to dismiss him or her from your school. Can you, without reservation, ensure that the traditional high school will better serve this student than the ECHS? It is a difficult "guarantee" for a school principal to make because the ECHS model inherently uses an individualized plan for each student.

To address this concern, we suggest that before this situation ever occurs, set up a protocol by which the situation is examined. One idea is to establish a committee of three to four people, and if possible, include the traditional high school principal (to whose campus you're considering as the destination for the problem student). Then, in a case-by-case basis, answer these three questions:

1. Define the behaviors that have brought the student to this committee.

2. Identify the academic successes and academic shortcomings of this student.

3. Using the answers to #1 and #2, identify what it is about the school where the child would be sent that would better serve him/her.

We have heard principals and teachers tell us that students were sent back to their traditional high school because, "He just couldn't pass the college classes," or, "She can't meet the standard on the entrance exam." If you now answer the three objective questions above, it will help you and your colleagues determine whether or not the student is better off remaining in your ECHS where *at least* he or she will earn a high school diploma and a little bit of college credit, and experience a whole lot of college culture. The point is that immature behavior, attention-seeking behavior, and the historic inability to fit into the public school system are contributing to many of the decisions that are made to send ECHS students away - and all of the reasons will continue to be an issue in a traditional school where that student will be more likely to fall through the cracks.

Structures need to be in place to efficiently implement the IEPs (individual education plans) for all students. Later in the chapter, you will see a completed crosswalk, or what we like to think of as the groundwork of an ECHS IEP.

Planning the Academic Sequence

The graphic below is an excellent planning tool for the Early College High School counselor. Its simplicity will truly allow you to plan the best roadmap for your school, providing a place to record the path to the high school diploma.

Subject area that has requirements for either degree	Taken in HS freshmen year	Taken in HS sopho-more year	Taken in HS junior year	Taken in HS senior year	Notes to further investigate
Science					
Social Studies					
Mathematics					
English					
Foreign Language					
Technology					
Physical Education					
Fine Arts					

At the same time, have the college counselor or liaison assemble the list of courses in the college's core curriculum that should be transferable to any state IHE (institute of higher education) *and* the requirements for the two most commonly earned associate's degrees. (Note: we know there are multiple degrees that can be earned and seem to realistically fit with the high school degree demands.) Remember, you are developing the road map that any early college high school student can take. When there are students with special skills or interests you will tweak their individual plans to the exact courses needed). When choosing the college courses, think of it like this: if you were advising two traditional college students that perhaps struggled in high school, what course track would you put them on?

In 2010 California established an Associate's Degree for Transfer through SB 1440. Among the benefits of this collaborative effort between the community college system and the California State University system is guaranteed acceptance to the four year college upon completion of this AA-T or AS-T (Associate's for Transfer) at the community college and the guarantee that no coursework would have to be repeated at the 4-year institution. And the intent is clear, as stated on the California Community College (2015) web page: *Even if you do not complete or have to delay finishing your bachelor's degree, you'll still have an associate degree and no one can take that from you.* It can significantly increase your earning potential and provide you with the skills employers are looking for in this difficult economy. Read more at http://tinyurl.com/zlxr2e3. This example serves as the kind of planning needed at the ECHS, using this structured requirement plan and determining how it matches with high school requirements.

From that list of college requirements, define the course offerings and provide the information in a document that is available to all stakeholders. The following page has a form that serves as a good example, and can even be a part of the articulation agreement between the college and the school district.

_____ ECHS with _____ COLLEGE
Dual Credit Courses
School Year: _____

Listed below are _____College's courses and their equivalent _____ school district course that can be taken for dual credit. If you wish to take a class not on the list, you must obtain written approval and an equivalent _____ school district course title from the ECHS principal before enrolling at _____ College. Students need to consult with a college/university advisor about transferability of courses.

COLLEGE	SCHOOL DISTRICT		CREDITS	PREREQ (COURSE OR ENTRACE EXAM)
ART				
ART 1301	SURVEY—ART HISTORY	8190 ART 3 HISTORY A	.5 CR	NONE
BUSINESS				PREREQ (COURSE OR ENTRACE EXAM)
TECH APPS				PREREQ (COURSE OR ENTRACE EXAM)
MATH				PREREQ (COURSE OR ENTRACE EXAM)

This form is available at www.echsguidebook.com.

Once you have this completed the worksheets, the crosswalk development begins. You want to plan a reasonable schedule for a *typical* ECHS student such that an associate's degree is attainable. Will every student reach this pinnacle? Historic data indicates that it is not likely. But even if only one-third earn the associate's degree, the other two-thirds are well ahead on the post-secondary path as compared to their traditional high school counterparts. You want to set the program up so that with the proper support, many students will earn the degree – like more than 60% did at San Antonio's Travis ECHS in 2014. Ironically, once you have a graduating class with a certain percentage earning college degrees, the general public, school district board of trustees, and other educators will want to know why all your students didn't earn the associate's! It is almost like they lose perspective and forget that the target population was classified "at risk" of not even finishing high school! As you approach the fourth year, you will truly want to think through this and prepare yourself with talking points for the various stakeholders (board members, civic organizations in your community, superintendent and central office staff, parents, community).

A bad trap to fall into is not planning for the entire four years. It is definitely easier to plan only the first and second years. We strongly encourage you to plan out two or three scenarios and sequences for the entire four or five year block rather than just looking at years one and two. Planning and adjusting creates a vision for you, your staff, the college, the parents, and the students. As we discussed in Students, Staff, and Other Stakeholders, there will be many people asking about the ECHS. Having a plan for all four or five years is vital.

It is very important that all courses in your side-by-side crosswalk are approved by both institutions' academic departments and recognized for dual credit. The college class will typically not change their syllabus, requirements, or student learning outcomes (SLOs), but the school district is still required to teach all of the student expectations designated for each course by your state education agency. For example, recent legislation in Illinois changed some requirements for social studies with specific recommendations including: *require a civic education in the high school, require a service learning project in middle and high school, and involve students in the election process* (Illinois Task Force, 2014). Early College High Schools in Illinois will have to ensure that their student meet these requirements, even if there is nothing existing in their scope and sequence prior to this ruling. That ECHS principal in Illinois will need to thoroughly examine the 'civic education' requirements, compare them to what the college offers in the existing government course, and make a plan to fulfill any requirements that are missing.

This is of particular concern if the ECHS students are taking a dual credit class for a course that is state-tested in high school. For example, in Texas many students qualify to take the introductory US History course in college. Like many states, Texas has an end of course standardized exam for US History. Carefully comparing the high school's Student Expectations (SEs) and the college's Student Learning Outcomes (SLOs) will ensure that the students are learning all the necessary information. Know that it is ultimately the responsibility of the ECHS administrator to monitor this, but the job of both partners to ensure the educational components are met. We encourage you to be proactive. Work with your liaison and deans to educate the college instructor about the requirements. Typically, the college instructor wants to fulfill the requirements, but also typically, he or she might not even be aware of them because it is not part of the existing course.

Once you determine the course work that will be offered to ECHS students, start thinking about the sequence of courses. Your college liaison and counselors will be able to help with the advice that is given to traditional students. There is an existing logical sequence, and it will be a good starting point. But remember to constantly consider the non-dual credit (traditional high school) course load already faced by your students as you make decisions about the sequence. Here are some options:

Option A   A common approach is for the liaison and ECHS administrator to choose two college courses that will be taken as a cohort by the freshmen class.   Typically, these are chosen from physical education, fine or performing arts classes, introductory psychology classes, communications (usually speech), health, and foreign languages, any of which will fulfill requirements for both the high school diploma and college degree. Remember to adhere to your IHE's requirements around entrance testing (example, many ECHSs include an introductory speech course for freshmen specifically because it does not have a testing requirement to take it). By taking the two classes as a cohort, the ECHS teachers are able to support the students during advisory period or other tutoring times. That support includes helping the students become familiar with the process of using the instructors' office hours, using the college writing center, and of course, traditional tutoring help.   What many ECHS faculty have seen is that the students have difficulty 1 - sitting for a 80-90 minute lecture; 2- filtering the information from the instructor during that lecture; and 3 - comprehending, note-taking, and information gathering from the textbook.   Start thinking about how to mitigate these deficits; more ideas will develop as you continue through the book.

And how you accommodate all students: In   addition   to what is listed in Option A, identify a small group of students that can handle one more dual credit class as freshmen. During summer bridge, administer your college partner's entrance exam (Accuplacer, Asset, Compass, or in Texas - TSI).   Most colleges clearly identify requirements for their courses (both entrance exam requirements and prerequisite coursework).   There are designated courses that have minimal requirements, and are often targeted for these first cohorts (and used as described in Option A).   In addition to the plan for Option A, identify the rising freshmen that are 1 - native Spanish (or another language) speakers and immediately enroll them in the appropriate college course (see your college partner's Office of Language Studies for more information on the testing or placement into language courses); and 2 - high achievers on the reading <u>and</u>

writing portions of the entrance exam, and have them take an introductory history, geography, sociology, or psychology course. In a cohort of 100 students, your native speakers of another language will be easy to predict; and your high achieving reading/writing students will likely number fewer than 10 (assuming your cohort is the true ECHS target population of students under-represented in college). <u>But remember, these students are exiting 8th grade. They still need academic support.</u> They very well may have been bored with 8th grade, found the curriculum repetitive, and thus lost touch with the skills needed for success or simply never learned what was needed to study when they didn't understand. Or perhaps they never experienced *not understanding*. Making the learning environment as supportive as possible will result in students that really recognize a love for learning.

> **If this is the first time that your college partner is involved with the early college program, be proactive and contact other ECHSs and their college partners to find out which courses they offer *before* freshmen meet the college entrance exam requirements. This will be an easy question for them to answer. Take advantage of the hundreds of ECHSs that have already traversed this path.**

A very important point to remember is that just because these students are high achievers, they will still need support, much like the native Spanish speakers who, also at age 14 or 15, will be in their first college class. Don't fall into the trap so many schools do where they consider gifted students, or native Spanish speakers taking Spanish class, don't need help with learning - they do! (Do we assume that are native English speakers never need help with English class?) Both groups will have success, as will your cohort that is taking a psychology or art history class together, but only with support from the staff. That includes the use of a college-readiness class which teaches them the college-level note taking, other information gathering skills, and writing skills they need, as well as rigorous social studies and English classes where their critical reading and analysis skills are pushed to high levels.

> The entire ECHS staff must take ownership in the success of the students in college classes—not just their course. What does this mean? Having conversations about their experiences in college classes and the workload, monitoring systems such as note taking, use of the syllabus, etc. Ask about projects and tests. Together, as a staff, determine what you all can do to help the adolescents in your school accelerate their 'college readiness' growth.

Finally, the macro-benefits of 10% of your students taking another college class provides evidence that the education plan is indeed individualized. When students are challenged, they enjoy being in school. Don't hold back your high achievers, or students like your native speakers whose skills are beyond what your school district curriculum offers. When students are bored and not engaged, they lose motivation. Also, remember that for every student taking, for example, college Spanish, you have fewer taking high school Spanish and thus a better teacher-student ratio in the high school classes.

Option B: Move directly to the individual education plans and allow students who reach the college entrance exam standard to move into classes on the college campus based on their needs. Give them some latitude in choosing a degree plan that might not as common. These qualifying students integrate into existing classes that traditional college student attend, and might need an even stronger support system than is described in Option A. While this is typical for the ECHS junior year, most schools do not choose to "dive" into Individual Education Plans (IEPs) with freshmen. Why? In Option A, the ECHS principal is talking with a handful of college instructors about the ins and outs of the program. Educating them on the design and intent of the model is much easier than educating all of the potential college instructors that Option B might include. Also, you will find that there are college instructors who simply never considered the possibility of 14 and 15 year olds in their classes, and simply will not have it. You cannot set your students up for this scenario. Imagine a high achieving, yet meek 15 year old girl who needs clarification about a writing assignment approaching an instructor who is retired from business and let's say, very 'old school' in approach to life and education. Most likely, the girl will not approach him, and if she does and receives an insensitive response, she might not ever again approach an instructor. Mitigating these kinds of situations is absolutely part of the process - as the ECHS administrator, the college administrators, and the liaison, you must find ways to be proactive and set the students up for success.

You will also have students that *do not* meet standard and thus take a full-time high school class load, or the cohort courses described in Option A. These students are common – remember, the target population is *at-risk*. That is they are at risk of not finishing high school. They have never had anyone challenge them, accelerate learning for them, or in some cases, believe in them.

Option B might be better served as the scenario for those few Early Colleges that are exclusively using online courses (often in remote areas of the country) and for those students you have determined already have the habits of mind and 'soft skills' to advocate for themselves as well as discipline themselves to succeed in the college setting.

Option C: The easiest way to control the college class is to have your high school teachers, who are accountable to the school district for their paycheck and thus directly to the ECHS principal, be the college instructors. With the proper credentials, typically a Master's Degree with a set number of hours in the discipline being taught, the college will credential adjunct instructors. Some school districts will even reimburse the teacher's tuition if they work toward that degree while employed. We highly recommend that this option is not utilized for the entire ECHS four-year sequence, and go further in stating that it NOT be used as the predominant way that students earn most of their college credits. Imagine a student attending an ECHS but never actually going to the college or interacting with traditional college students and more importantly, sitting before traditional college instructors. Even an ECHS situated on a college campus can create a situation where the students never leave the 'nest.' The ECHS model is designed to address the need for more students, traditionally underrepresented in college, to be successful pursing a bachelor's degree. If you provide 50% or more of the classes in a controlled environment that looks far more like the high school than the college, how will the students grow into college students? What components will you put into place to replicate the accountability and culture? What happens when your school district and college have conflicting policies. For example, it is not uncommon for a school district to require a large number of graded assignments - let's say 20 in a nine week cycle, while a typical college class has 4 or 5 graded assignments? Ask yourself, "Is my school truly preparing the students for the demands of the four-year university?" These are the kinds of questions that need to be considered.

> At the end of the semester, have the students calculate their high school grades using only major tests, papers, and projects. Because most high school teachers include homework, quizzes, and sometimes class work, in the grade, high school grades tend to be higher than the average of tests and projects. By having them go through this exercise, they are introduced to the grading system in college, the process opens up conversations about *why* note taking, studying, and reading are important.

Student Enrollment

Early College High School students are enrolled in the college and the school district. They should have college identification (ID) badges that are recognized by all school district personnel, which is especially important in the school-within-a-school setting. It is preferable to choose this option of one ID badge for the obvious reasons like cost of replacement when lost, but more importantly for the beginning of the culture-building that is imperative to the success of the program. While more of a symbol in years 1 and 2, the badge is a <u>college</u> ID. This is a unique group who ventured away from the safety of the familiar traditional school. It's almost like a badge of honor.

During summer bridge camp, plan time to complete the parts of the enrollment process for which students must be present. This varies by institution, from some colleges using the data from the school district to enroll the students (thus the students are not present), to completing the application form online so the data base can recognize the students and assign a student ID number. Whatever the procedure, know it well and plan for it. And be realistic about the amount of time this will take. Think about moving students through these registration-like processes in groups of 10-15 so that the others are actively engaged in other necessary and meaningful activities, rather than sitting around waiting. Remember - they are eighth graders! No one likes to stand in line, and time is precious – again, you are preparing them to possibly be full time college students at 16 years of age. As the ECHS administrator, do a practice run or simulation. One new ECHS had been very proactive about setting up the ECHS, but when it came to registration, the college partner had not added the new 'high school' to the list of dual credit high school in their database. The staff person actually doing the registration on the computer (for the college) did not know about the ECHS. All of the students were registered for dual credit at their home high school (or the high school they would have attended had they not chosen to go to the ECHS).

As college students, the ECHS cohort should have full access to all college programs and services. With that comes the responsibility of the ECHS staff and liaison to educate each cohort about the differences among 1 - their middle school experience, 2 - their perception of the high school experience, and 3 - the reality of the college campus. Keep in mind, few 14 or 15 year olds have perceptions of college - they simply haven't even thought about it because it was always so very far away. In many cases, no one has asked them questions like, "What do you think it will be like to use the college writing center? What exactly happens when you plaigerize?" The choice to enroll in an ECHS has accelerated college entrance from 4 to 5 years away to now! Thus, spend time touring the campus, discussing behavior expectations, introducing them to all kinds of workers at the college, integrating them with some traditional college students, and repeatedly discussing the mature behavior that is expected of them.

Adolescents, like adults, tend to better meet expectations once they know what the expectations are. That sounds obvious, but there are too many instances where students simply don't understand the expectations. Like you did with behavior expectations, have clear discussions about the actual course load for the next four years; and be sure to introduce both early and revisit them often. Individual graduation plans that outline both courses at the college/university and high school must be developed in collaboration with the school district counselor who is also well versed in the college requirements. Students must be able to meet all the requirements of the state graduation plan *as well as* the college's core curriculum requirements. Typically, during the first two years, students are registered for their university classes by the high school counselor. Once they become high school juniors, they are taught how to navigate the registration process and are allowed to register themselves for college courses. This is extremely important because more than just earning an associate's degree, we want the students to be experienced and confident when they go to the four-year university. Counselors should monitor this process closely. In some cases, the colleges may set aside a few spaces and allow the high school students to register early, much like a privileged group of athletes or academic scholarship winners would be. The following template was developed by Pam Geissinger-Sandy, the counselor at the ECHS at Brookhaven in Farmer's Branch, Texas. The one-page design is easy for students, parents, and teachers to use, and the basis of the worksheets in the previous chapter.

The text is color coded on the actual form used by the ECHS at Brookhaven. This is available at echsguidebook.com.

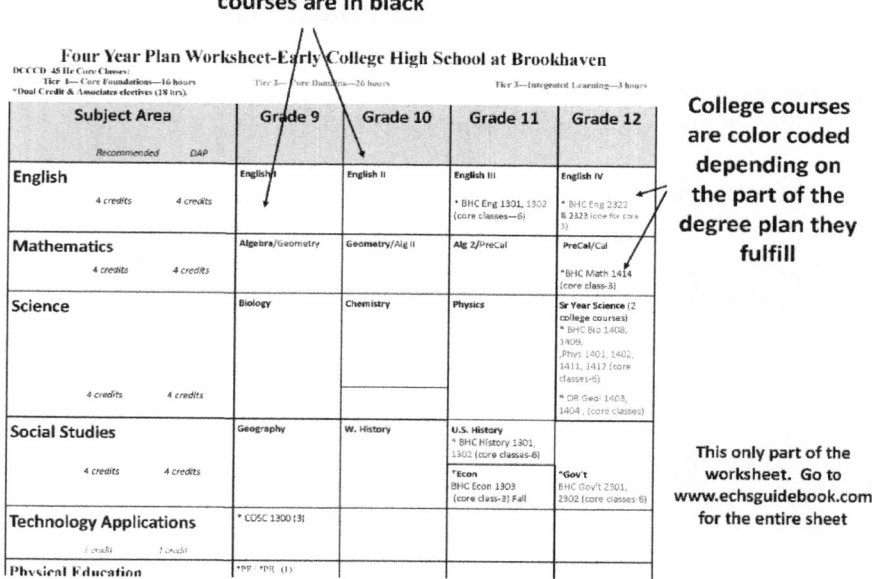

Created by Pam Geissinger-Sandy of Carrollton Farmers Branch ISD while counselor at ECHS at Brookhaven

Dropping a Course

Don't allow students to drop a college course without visiting with the ECHS counselor or principal. The school counselor has developed an individual graduation plan for each student, and they need to be required to discuss interventions prior to dropping a course. (This is a good example of support needed to help students navigate the college process. A traditional college student can drop courses without any counseling, often wasting money and time. By meeting with a counselor, students will reflect on *why* the course should be dropped and further examine the implications of the action.) We have seen examples where ECHS students, sometimes at the direction of the college instructor, have gone to the registrar and dropped the course, never telling anyone at the ECHS! How will the principal or counselor know? And does the student know that by taking this task on he potentially risks not even earning his high school diploma? Be sure that this rule is steadfast in their minds, and if possible, spend time at the registrar's office to see if there is a way to code students "ECHS" and send a flag email any time one tries to drop a course. Computers are amazing, and this is a very realistic intervention.

As an ECHS administration and staff, work together to develop a process for students to drop a college course. Yes, each cohort is a group of students that are statistically less likely to even go to college after high school graduation! How can we not drop them from college classes if it is necessary? What you need to do is define, "necessary," well before the first student ever enters your door with such a request. There are multiple benefits to this: you and your staff will truly think through what the first college class experience will be like, and as importantly, what scaffolds you can put into place to help students avoid failures.

Master Schedule

Ideally, the master schedule will match that of your higher education partner. The benefits might not seem necessary during the initial year when your students are taking one or two college classes, but in the big picture, it will be a huge logistical benefit as your ECHS progresses. Among the easiest advantages to recognize is that when students take college classes, having the same start and end times is needed to allow for the quantity of classes in a day. (So if your start time for first period is 8:30 am and the college starts at 8:00, how will you ensure that the student is there on time?) Additionally, it establishes the expectation that college is part of every student's life, and in Early College High Schools, that expectation starts in 9th grade! Thus, the college-going culture begins. Finally, most schools move to the college's schedule by Year 3. By starting in Year 1, the stakeholders (principals, teachers, counselors and students) can transition with support - believe it or not, you have time in Year 1; and in Year 3, you'll have three cohorts, more work with the college, and possibly less control over those juniors!

What is not so easy to embrace without careful consideration is the choice of using only block schedule. The shift to 80 or 90-minute classes is not without challenges, and some schools have truly found a nice mix of block and shorter classes based on the needs of the students. The following information will help you make an informed decision.

Year by Year

~~Assumption~~ Fact: No college is going to change their schedule to accommodate a school district's schedule.

Questions to ask yourself as you develop the master schedule. There are no wrong or right answers, but if you fail to consider each of these points, you will likely have issues at some point in the future. (And really put these answers on paper. It is easy to skim past them, but they truly all need attention if you are in your planning year.)

1. What are the pros and cons of following the IHE (institute of higher education) schedule in Year 1 and 2?

28

2. What are the pros and cons of following the IHE schedule in Years 3 and beyond?

3. If/when we move to a 90-minute block, like the college, how will I prepare my teachers for the transition? How will I prepare my students? How will I prepare the parents? Does it affect bus schedules? Cafeteria schedules? Other school wide systems?

4. Is it possible to use one schedule for freshmen and sophomores and another for juniors and seniors?

5. Do I need to build formal time into the school day to scaffold the transition to a more rigorous schedule? To build endurance for 90 minute classes? What does that look like? Why am I doing it?

6. How adept are my teachers at fully utilizing the longer class period schedule, including incorporating typically non-sequenced objectives and not wasting instructional time? If they need help with this, do I have a way to help them?

When designing the master schedule, you might find that matching the college schedule is preferable. If you don't, it is likely that in the middle of Year 3 you'll ask yourself why you didn't choose the college schedule in Year 1.

For those using the school within a school model, there are even more challenges. Administrators need to answer the following questions before developing the master schedule:

7. Students WILL need tutoring. What happens if that student is a cheerleader or basketball player that will need to miss practice (or part of practice) in order to fulfill his tutoring requirement?

8. Where and with whom will students eat lunch? If it is with the rest of the student body, experience suggests that it will be problematic. Issues around grades, homework, and class work, lead to misinformation spiraling throughout the school and neighborhood.

9. Where are the ECHS classrooms? They need to be clustered together in an area of the building that is not used by the traditional school.

10. Who will teach the ECHS electives? Ideally, ECHS cohorts will have electives together. But most districts that choose the school within a school model allow students to participate on athletic teams, band, choir, etc. Those activities must fall at a time that does not conflict with the college classes. Thus, the ECHS administrator must secure a timeframe for cohort classes *before the master schedule is developed.*

Still focused on the master schedule, know that as challenging as year 1 seems, it is nothing like years 3, 4, and beyond. Mentioned above, you lose more control over the schedule - your cohort 1 students are in 1, 2, 3, or maybe even 4 college classes as high school juniors - and they're in a lot of different courses. You likely have 65% of cohort 2 working on college classes together, 10% taking three college classes independently of peers, and the remainder haven't met the necessary college entrance exam standard, thus needing their high school credits to be offered by your staff. And what about your newest group, cohort 3?...all freshmen, are now on a full block and their high school teachers have no experience with it (because during years 1 and 2, a 60-minute class period was used every day). You are busy running around keeping up with it all and can't take the time to help them transition to teaching in a 90 minute block.

Let's look at why you might consider the college schedule right away:

Recommendation: Keep freshmen in cohorts for
this first year in college.

During Years 1 and 2, many ECHSs keep freshmen and sophomores in cohorts because they will take essentially, the same course work. By using the cohort system with one or a few college instructors, you are attempting to scaffold the higher education experience by at least keeping peer groups of rookies together. For the principal, working with 2 – 3 college instructors is very manageable. But the full staff will support the transition. If a small percentage of the cohort is able to take additional courses, absolutely allow that. But they are still part of the cohort, say for *Speech* class, as in the example provided.

Recommendation: As much as possible, match IHE
systems that involve your school including the schedule.

Colleges are not changing their schedules to accommodate the ECHS or any dual credit program. Look both at the college's weekly schedule (do classes meet Monday, Wednesday, Friday or do they meet Monday, Wednesday only?) and the daily schedule (80 minute classes? 90 minutes?). If your college partner utilizes both 60 and 90 minute classes, you will want to do that too.

By having the ECHS high school classes use a schedule similar to the college, you are eliminating one barrier to success – the ability to sustain learning for an 80-90 minute period. They will learn in a lower-stakes environment. You do not want your 14-year-old students' first experience in a 90 minute class to be with a college instructor (who also may be teaching 14-year old for the very first time!). The students are developing the skills (note-taking, focus, extracting important information, identifying what to work on outside of class, learning *how* to work outside of class, prioritizing study time, using a calendar to plan study time and record assignments, etc.) with your high school teachers who have a better understanding of where the students came from (middle school). Typically, the college instructors expect them to know these "soft skills," because a *typical* college student is 18 or 19 years old. By working on these competencies in summer bridge and concurrently in the semester, you're equipping the students with what David Conley refers to as *academic behaviors*. He states, "...academic success requires the mastery of key skills necessary to comprehend material and complete academic tasks successfully, and the nature of college learning in particular requires that significant amounts of time be devoted to learning outside of class for success to be achieved in class" (Conley, 2007).

Recommendation: Work closely and purposefully with your IHE partner in identifying instructors for your freshmen and sophomores.

One of the biggest challenges experienced by new early colleges involves the adults - finding the *right* college instructor that understands that these are <u>capable</u> 14-year-olds, but still ....well, 14 years old! Many principals can tell stories of woe. And even the most proactive of ECHS principals – those who have one-on-one conversations with each instructor well before they ever teach a cohort of new ECHS students – find that there is nothing like that first semester of teaching a freshmen level ECHS cohort to truly understand.

"The Computer Information Systems instructor came into our first cohort class - a group of 25 freshmen. She, told the students to open to page 35 and do what was in the book on their computer. She then sat at her computer station, never modeling or interacting with the students."

---first year ECHS Principal

"The instructor distributed the syllabus and never referenced it again. He lectured on topics other than those covered in the readings, and on the first test, the students were STUNNED to see so much from the book." *--3rd year ECHS Principal*

Recommendation

Recommendation: Develop a strong relationship with your liaison and deans.

While you cannot control the human resources department of the college, you can control the duties of the school district staff. If you have the human resources allocation, have a school district teacher, counselor, or other staff member go to class with the cohort - even if it is just for 5-6 class meetings initially. That adult serves as the cohort's advocate in a proactive manner. Meeting the instructor a few days before classes start to give context to the role will almost always be well received. A good icebreaker is to be sure the college instructor knows that he or she is serving underrepresented students - the term *early college* often connotes the vision of 'academically advanced' students. We have repeatedly heard college instructors say, "I thought these students were gifted," or "I thought they were supposed to be ready for college." Here are three examples of how this can work, but you must build in the structure during Year 0 (planning year):

> *GOOD: I work at the ECHS and am serving as your class liaison. Please email me with any information at all that will help the students succeed. Like you, we want them to work hard, learn and excel. Since they are 14, they need a bit more support and one of my duties is to be sure that I know what the requirements, assignments, etc. are for your class. How can we work together so I can fulfill my district obligation while supporting you and the students?*

> *BETTER: I work at the ECHS and I'm sure you know that your M,W,F 10:30 am class is a group of high school freshmen embarking on their very first college class. As you can imagine, we'll have students that will have no problem keeping up with your pace, but since they are coming right from middle school where the demands aren't typically as rigorous as even high school, I just want to be sure they stay on track in the beginning. Please utilize me as needed - email me if you think I can help; our belief is that if I can sit and listen to you during their class, then I can ask the students the right questions when we're back on the ECHS campus - the kinds of things an 18 or 19-year-old already knows to ask him/herself.*

> *The BEST situation is to use the language from the BETTER example above, and also diplomatically convey the information about the provision in the MOU that requires the college instructor to communicate with the principal or the liaison including sending a report to that person or the principal with*

mid-term grades, itemized. Thus, consider adding this to your MOU! There is nothing like agreed upon written documentation (signed by executives of the organizations in the MOU) to help assuage the potential confrontational situation.

Consider the three scenarios above and how they truly communicate the importance of thinking through the very new college/ECHS interactions. As a PLC, you want to mitigate problems much like parents want to provide support without 'doing the work' for the students. You want to help put systems in place, like the grade checks, so the students 'earn' the grades and you perhaps push them to study, take notes, organize their notes, and take care of outside work like language labs. Brainstorm other ideas where you can help your students both have success and learn to eventually navigate college on their own.

Example of a Master Schedule
Below is the Monday/Wednesday/Friday schedule

MON, WED, FRI SCHEDULE							
TEACHER	1ST	2ND		3RD	4TF	5TH	
	8:00—9:15	9:20—10:35	11:00—11:30	10:40—12:35	12:40—1:55	2:00—3:15	3:20—3:45
ELA TEACHER 1	ENGLISH I	ENGLISH 3	LUNCH	PLANNING	ENGLISH 3	ENGLISH 1	ADVISORY
ELA TEACHER 2	ENGLISH — 10TH GRADE	ENGLISH 2— 9TH GRADE	LUNCH	PLANNING	ENGLISH 2— 9TH GRADE	ENGLISH 2— 10TH GRADE	ADVISORY
MATH TEACHER 1	ALGEBRA 1	ALGEBRA 2	LUNCH	ALGEBRA 1	PLANNING	ALGEBRA 1	ADVISORY
MATH TEACHER 2	GEOMETRY— 10TH GRADE	GEOMETRY— 9TH GRADE	LUNCH	GEOMETRY— 9TH GRADE	PLANNING	GEOMETRY— 10TH GRADE	ADVISORY
SS TEACHER 1	WORLD GEOGRAPHY	PLANNING	LUNCH	WORLD GEOGRAPHY	WORLD GEOGRAPHY	WORLD GEOGRAPHY	ADVISORY
SS TEACHER 2	WORLD HISTORY	PLANNING	LUNCH	WORLD HISTORY	WORLD HISTORY	WORLD HISTORY	ADVISORY
SCIENCE TEACHER 1	PLANNING	BIOLOGY	LUNCH	BIOLOGY	BIOLOGY	BIOLOGY	ADVISORY
SCIENCE TEACHER 2	PLANNING	CHEMISTRY	LUNCH	CHEMISTRY	CHEMISTRY	CHEMISTRY	ADVISORY
FOREIGN LANGUAGE	CHINESE 1	SPANISH 1	LUNCH	SPANISH 2	SPANISH 2	PLANNING	ADVISORY
COLLEGE PREP TEACHER	COLLEGE PREP CLASS	COLLEGE PREP CLASS	LUNCH	COLLEGE PREP CLASS	COLLEGE PREP CLASS	PLANNING	ADVISORY

Notice that above is the schedule for Monday, Wednesday, and Friday. The class periods above correspond to the full week schedule on the next page. So ELA Teacher 1 has 4th period students from 12:40 - 1:55 on M,W,F and on Thursday from 8:00 - 9:15. The Tuesday and Thursday mornings are equally distributed among the class periods. This, developed and used by Usamah Rodgers when she opened Cedar Hill Collegiate, an ECHS south of Dallas, does an excellent job of balancing minutes among all classes. The schedule is strictly used for 9th and 10th grades with all students in the same cohort because the college partner is located more than 10 miles from ECHS campus. The 11th and 12th graders are housed on the college campus with 3-4 ECHS faculty where they follow the college schedule.

ECHS BELL SCHEDULE

	1ST	2ND	LUNCH	3RD	4TH	5TH	6TH	7TH	ADVISORY
MON, WED, FRI	8:00—9:15	9:20—10:35	11:00—11:30	10:40—12:35	12:40—1:55	2:00—3:15			3:20—3:45
TUESDAY	8:00—9:15	9:20 - 10:35	11:00—11:30	10:40—12:25			12:30—1:55	2:00—3:20	3:20—3:45
THURSDAY			11:00—11:30		8:00—9:15	9:20—10:35	12:30—1:55	2:00—3:20	3:20—3:45

THURSDAY CLUBS 10:35—11:00   TUTORIALS/STUDY HALL 11:30—12:25

The benefits of this schedule for student success include:

- Relatively equal amount of seat time in each school district class
- College classes clustered (periods 6 and 7)
- 75-minute classes with high school teachers
- Advisory time
- Clubs (National Honor Society, Student Council, academic competitions, debate, soccer, etc.)
- Preparation and registration for SAT and ACT can be worked into the non-academic pieces in the schedule*

*The non-academic pieces include, but are not limited to, communicating necessary information to students about college registration, school district benchmarks, college honor society, field trips, school dances, community service opportunities, etc. The list is unique to each school, but there is time allocated in the master schedule so that instruction time is not lost.

The benefits of this schedule <u>for teacher growth</u> include:

- Common planning with the other teacher in the department
- Thursday after lunch is allocated for professional development of all instructional staff while the students are in their cohort college classes

Designing the master schedule so that the instructional block (be it 60, 75 or 90 minutes) is <u>only for instruction</u> is another important asset that you *can* control. Your teachers will appreciate it! Consider building a 20-minute homeroom or advisory period that meets once or twice each week. BUT, do not build it without clear intent on how to use it (see questions below). Many schools include a blanket 'advisory' and task teachers, instructional coaches, and/or assistant principals with developing curriculum for that time. Too often that occurs 'on the fly,' or at the last minute simply because there are other issues that are more pressing (like lesson plans for the academic classes). Administrative issues are part of the system - build time for those things to be taken care of. It will reduce frustration among the teachers who worry about instruction time.

Ask yourself the following question: *What kinds of administrative demands must be accomplished in a semester?*

These might include:

a. Forms - Free and Reduced Lunch, Contests, central office surveys
b. One-time (or maybe not!) issues: ID badges, library cards
c. Counselor needs: Graduation plans, information about report cards
d. Community service information, planning, and tracking

Philosophically, including all adults on campus as part of the advisory team results in buy-in from staff, relationship building to a deeper level with students in a low-stakes environment, and a lower staff-student ratio during advisory. So include all staff. But consider the following: What about staff members that are only on campus part time? How will that impact the advisory time? In fact, they need the time with students more than anyone, but monies might prohibit that from working, especially if you are paying by time on campus.

> **STRUCTURE**   pronunciation: strək(t)SHər
> According to GOOGLE: the arrangement of and relations
> between the parts or elements of something complex.
> For this book: school wide support
>
> **SYSTEM**   pronunciation: sistəm
> According to GOOGLE: a set of principles or procedures
> according to which something is done; an organized
> scheme or method.
> For this book: individual classroom supports

Chapter 3 - Student Support Structures

The design of early college high school is meant to support student success. The partnership with the college is an integral part of the design, and services provided by both the school district and college will collectively make the early college work. To make the lives of the students 'work,' it is important to also involve the parents and guardians. At the very least, systems to communicate with parents must be in place and understood by all parties; at best, the parents are partners in the successful education of their children.

Since the ECHS students are just beginning to experience college courses, it is important that academic structures are in place to support students. For the purposes of this book, structures are school-wide support, and systems are used in individual classrooms. Most schools include structures like tutoring, mentoring, and special classes to support learning (both credit bearing and non-credit bearing) classes.

Special Classes

Among the most popular special classes is a **freshmen level college skills support class**. The name of the course and the high school credit awarded vary from state to state, as well as within schools in each state. Some colleges offer their non-credit earning college support class, while others offer a non-core course for credit. An additional option is to utilize the AVID (Advancement Via Individual Determination) program. Whether created by our district, your college partner, the AVID system, or a new unique course designed specifically for your ECHS, we strongly recommend that all early college high schools include this course, and investigate which path is best for your students. By dedicating a class period to this support, you are making it clear to parents, students, the community, and the college that you are serious about the success of the students.

One thing that is often a challenge for the ECHS is to design the class to balance support for the freshmen in both their high school courses and their college courses. It is not as simple as using the same model that your traditional high school uses – their students have different academic demands. Additionally, purposeful work needs to be done to help the students develop into self-responsible students at a much earlier age than in a traditional high school. Take time as a staff to determine how to best utilize this precious time.

1. Identify the key skills and content knowledge that must be mastered by the end of the freshmen year and list them for the group to see.

2. Create groupings from that list with logical sequences. For example, *speaking respectfully to peers and adults, speaking appropriately in collaborative groups, modeling speaking for future cohorts, delivering a 5-minute speech in a classroom setting,* and *appropriately responding in the high school and college class setting* would be

grouped together because they all involve a form or degree of public speaking.

3. Work from the goal date (ex: end of freshmen year) as your starting point to the first day of summer bridge (before freshmen year) and place each in logical or purposeful order. You will definitely need to prioritize based on the demands faced chronologically. Using the speech example, the following might be the time frames (listed chronologically but planned with the end in mind):

   a. Summer bridge: Activity on appropriate interactions with adults and peers; introduction of the use of roles in collaborative group work; mini-play of college class scenarios.

   b. September – November: Collaborative group work in every class with roles requiring all students to speak at least three times in all classes at least once each week. December – May: at least twice each week.

   c. September – the college support class reviews summer bridge speech concepts; practices interactions in college class (role play).

   d. October and November: 2-minute speech in English and science classes.

   e. December – 2-3 minute speech in elective class.

   f. January – self-record speech on *What I love best about my ECHS.* (use the best for recruiting!)

   g. February – 3-minute speech in math class.

   h. March – Write an expository paper about how to give a 3-minute speech.

    i.   April – 5-minute speech in social studies class, recorded and included in student's portfolio.

    j.   May – work with parents, administrators, teachers from other schools to set up mock interviews or any academic conversation (ex: parents could hear about the challenges of the college class; administrators in the district could hear about the advantages of Early College)

4. Repeat the process for the other skill and content pieces. As you can see, it is a process that will take 3 – 4 hours to complete, but it will be well worth it.

Some veteran early colleges approach support classes more on an individualized basis. Victory Early College High School in the Aldine Independent School District in Houston has struggling students take **specialty study skills classes**, and if needed, take test preparation classes. Through the leadership of principal, Dr. Phyllis Cormier, the school has truly developed a culture of individualized learning plans in a coherent instructional setting. For example, shared with us by teacher Scott Groen, Victory staff are identifying students who need a sort of intervention because, while TSI-met (Texas' college entrance exam), there are still concerns among staff about the true readiness of the students for college classes. So a kind of 'soft-skills meetings' are now added to the many supports that are purposefully included at Victory ECHS.

If you are considering in a more specialized plan, use data to help you in the process. The next graphic shows a worksheet and a sample of a completed plan on the cohort's college entrance exam scores. Because college classes have different requirements (example, in order to take the college's Introduction to Composition, it is typically *not* necessary to have passed the math portion of Acculplacer, Compass, or TSI).

Individualized College Classes Plan

% of freshmen cohort that passed parts of tests indicated				Freshmen Year - 4 one-semester electives	
	Reading	Writing	Math	Courses they will take at college	Elective in ECHS
10%	x	x	x	Speech, Art History, Intro Sociology	none
13%	x	x		Speech, Art History	Alg 1 extra block
18%	x			Speech, Intro Sociology	Writer's Workshop
17%		x		Speech, PE	Critical Reading
5%		x	x	Speech, PE	Critical Reading
5%	x		x	Speech, PE	Writer's Workshop
32%				Speech, PE	Back to Basics Course

You'll notice that each horizontal line represents a percentage of the freshmen cohort. The last two columns show the electives they will take - 2 per semester - based on need. Those who pass all three parts most likely do not need the same support class that a student who passes one part needs. Thus the academically stronger student takes four college classes. The 17% who didn't pass math or reading along with the 5% that didn't pass only the reading section take two college classes plus a high school critical reading course, typically taught by your English teacher.

This example takes some work, and it can be implemented in the cohort's sophomore or junior year, after they have taken the freshmen support class. Or use it in the freshmen year if that makes sense. The intent of including it here is that this purposeful use of data to guide decision making supports the individualized instruction all educators hope for and early colleges value.

Next is a blank worksheet to replicate and revise, based on your school:

WORKSHEET

% of freshmen cohort that passed parts of tests indicated			Freshmen Year - 4 one-semester electives	
Reading	Writing	Math	Courses they will take at college	Elective in ECHS
X	X	X		none
X	X			Alg 1 extra block
X				Writer's Workshop
	X			Critical Reading
	X	X		Critical Reading
X		X		Writer's Workshop
				Back to Basics Course

Another class that is often set up to support students is **an 'off-day' study class** where an ECHS school district teacher supports the work of the college instructor. For example, if 20 sophomore students attend a college history class on Monday, Wednesday and Friday, the school district teachers will provide support classes during that time frame on Tuesday and Thursday. These support classes will provide students with assistance on homework, assignments, and guidance on how to grapple with difficult readings or concepts, and coaching on important research and study skills, such as note-taking and reading for understanding. There are repeated examples throughout the country, but most notable is the emergence of supporting students who embark on their first online college course. Computer based learning is a reality and should absolutely be a requirement of every high school student. But, like anything new, the students, regardless of age, need support. In Presidio Early College High School, geographically situated in a remote part of West Texas, all college classes are currently taken online. During that time, teachers are assigned to a group of students to ensure that they are working through assignments, listening to podcasts and live webcasts, completing projects, and receiving other needed support. In Roscoe, Texas, a town of fewer than 2000 people and located 90 minutes from Midland, teachers at the ECHS monitor the students in their content areas. The students take online college coursework and the teachers circulate through the room as the students traverse their coursework online, provide tutoring based on the needs of the group or individual. When the students view live lessons from their college instructors at a faraway location, the ECHS teacher watches as well, thus providing support in both better understanding content, adherence to deadlines for assignments, and skill development on filtering which content is important and will likely be on the test.

As you can see, there are a variety of ways classes can support the emerging college students and examining the needs of your campus is the best way to approach the task. Here are some questions to help you work through the process:

1. Where in your master schedule can you allow for a freshmen support class (in other words, how many electives will your freshmen be able to take including this course)?

2. Does the class need to meet every day?

3. Who will teach the class? Some schools have one teacher that teaches all students. Others train all teachers in the support pieces that will be used, and every teacher has one section. The philosophy for this choice is that teachers are more likely to implement the support systems if they are also teaching them (ex: Cornell Notes). The downside is that, like anything, you will have 'rock star' teachers and you will have struggling teachers. Only through high expectations and standards emphasizing the importance of this class will all teachers provide adequate support (meaning that no, your

chemistry class is not more important than this support class; they are equally important).

4. What skills will be developed? Whether in the designated class or in the academic classes, be sure to stick to the plan. Soft skills like note taking, use of a binder or other system, ability to filter lecture information, how to talk to peers, how to talk to instructors, and how to self-advocate are among the most common. Organized content tutoring is also common in these classes.

5. How will the classes be grouped? Many ECHSs find that they have a group of freshmen that have already completed Algebra 1 and/or ELA 1 in eighth grade. Do you cohort those students together because it is the only opportunity to support them in their respective mathematics classes (and possibly different college classes because they are most likely to be in more than one college class)? Do you truly randomize the students? This is a good idea if you find that your curriculum is more geared toward skill development than content tutoring. Do you rank the students by their scores in mathematics or English so that those who struggle the most in the respective subjects are assigned to your math and English teachers? If you look back at your answers to #4, it might help you make a decision on grouping.

6. Will there be a typical numeric grade for this class and if so, what comprises the grade? Remember, this course is designed to be a support course. Creating a situation where the students have even more classes is not a good idea. Think about the typical freshmen taking 5 high school credits (mathematics, social studies, English, science, and one elective) as well as one or two college courses. That is 7 credits. That is a full load of classes and more importantly, it is at a higher level of rigor than most students see in a regular high school class and definitely more rigorous than their middle school experiences. Truly use the class as a support and consider, if your district

allows, credit with pass/fail. Coincidentally, this option will also introduce the students to courses where pass/fail is the grading system, something most will run into sometime in their post-secondary career.

7. What curriculum will be used? Though you do not want to add more work, you do want to use the time wisely. Like in any class, there needs to be a curriculum and the teacher must do lesson plans. The curriculum needs to be around the habits of mind that need development.

8. What academic content support will the class need? AVID uses outside tutors who are typically paid between $9 - $15 per hour. Do you have the budget for that? If not using AVID, does the program you are using consider tutors? Does the college have a program where their undergraduate teaching assistants can be employed at the expense of the college? Are there volunteer tutors among retired teachers groups in the area? Are there juniors and seniors at your district's traditional high school who can serve as tutors for service hours?

Remember, this class is a safe-haven; a place where students want to be. At the same time, it is maintains the high expectations for the school, and serves as the glue that holds this academic challenge together for the students.

Tutoring

The structured tutoring program of the college has proven beneficial to young students attending early college high schools. Students can seek the assistance of specialized centers such as writing centers or math camps to help with assignments assigned by the higher ed instructors. As highlighted in Book 1: Partnerships and the MOU, these existing college support structures are available to your ECHS students. Listen to Yvette Cavazos, founding principal of Achieve ECHS in McAllen, Texas, at http://tinyurl.com/zax7f7s as she describes the great benefits of their partnership with South

Texas College.

On the school district side, it is likely that your teachers will have experience providing tutoring within a traditional school setting. BUT their experiences with tutoring are varied. The principal needs to provide guidance. For example, an ECHS might require teachers to use different instructional strategies in the tutoring session than those used in class. While this might be obvious, many, many teachers make the mistake of instructing the same way, the way that, well....didn't work in the large class setting. Ask your teachers to think about the following:

- Who needs to come to tutoring? How do you identify these students? (It needs to be for academic help and not behavioral issues – that needs to be addressed, but not in tutoring.)
- How will you identify the specific skills that need development? For example, students rarely are confused by ALL of the pieces of a lesson or content on a test. What data will you use to focus in on the real deficit? And most tutoring is around skills, not content mastery.
- What strategies will be used to reach the learner in this small group setting? And based on experience, ask math teachers, what will you do if the tutoring session is too large?
- Is tutoring punitive? Do the students feel like it is? If that is the case, talk about it at a PLC meeting.

Maximizing instructional time is the goal and reflective processes, such as thinking about these questions, truly create the structures for a successful school. If the teachers aren't thinking about these on their own, the principal's responsibility is to ask these kinds of questions.

Mentoring

MENTOR pronunciation: men̩tôr
An experienced and trusted advisor

Mentoring has also proved to be a very successful component of early college high school, but often not implemented due to the time commitment necessary to sustain the program. In practice, a staff member must recruit and identify mentors, ensure background checks are done, provide orientation to them, and continually monitor, to a degree, the work. Students are assigned a mentor, and in some cases this can include college and university staff. The role of the mentor is to meet regularly with the students to discuss progress, grades, and challenges. The benefits of the program will become clear as students reflect on the experiences. Their stories are powerful and amazing.

Existing schools have variations of mentoring programs that involve their own staff. Often, all members on staff (including the non-teaching staff) will be assigned an equal number of students. Staff members then monitor all academic progress and make frequent contacts with their students, with informal questions in the hallway (*Juanita - how is your research paper for Ms. Walker going?*) to ensuring their paperwork is completed to take the SAT or attend a school-sponsored college visit. Other teachers approach a student's mentor (Mr. Smith - is Juanita yours? Could you remind her about math tutoring?)

Tutors and mentors sometimes come from outside the staff. In order to successfully implement such a program, the principal will have to assign a staff member to coordinate it. Nothing is worse than losing volunteers due to lack of organization. But before embarking on either program, be sure to know the goals you have in mind. It is important to communicate them. For example, if the goal of the mentorship program is 1 - to expose students to professional role models and 2 - to expose students to professions with which they may be unfamiliar, then you will want to target some unique professions. For example, the city or county where you live will have planners, finance managers, code enforcement, and other public works jobs that aren't often well known to the typical teenager. The health care profession has radiologists, occupational therapists, and phlebotomists. If you can target other public agencies, you may find success in recruiting mentor volunteers. Many large private companies have full departments dedicated to outreach and volunteerism, and often those large companies express frustration when trying to help local education agencies.

It is highly advisable to structure an outside program for the students. The community and parents want to be involved, and with the goal of college readiness foremost in the design, finding professionals working in close proximity will yield great benefits for students. This might be a mentoring program to acquaint students with the kinds of jobs they show interest in.

Service Learning

Another idea is to include service learning in the students' four-year plan. Quest ECHS in Humble, Texas, has refined the process, serving as a model for all smaller academies. Their service learning program began before the school was even an Early College. Their service learning coordinator helps place *every* student into a position on Fridays (at which time the faculty can work together in PLCs, professional development, or planning). Learn more about this from Quest's Service Learning Coordinator at http://tinyurl.com/zmqgowb. Caldwell Early College High School has a YouTube video describing their school including service learning with students helping elementary children in their district and working at a soup kitchen.

Volunteering

Recently, while consulting at a new ECHS, the principal commented on the financial challenge around securing and paying for a school bus to take the students to volunteer at a community shelter. With school districts across the country tightening their budgets, creative solutions to service learning might lie in doing work on campus, inviting other groups to come to your school. For example, we once participated in a family game day with children from a homeless shelter that were transported by the shelter to the church. It is possible that your local boys and girls' club might be interested in doing the same for a structured activity with your students. Another idea is to contact the coordinator of large events like 5K runs or professional conferences to learn if there are opportunities to help by assembling the bags with advertisers' information or the envelopes that contain the participants' registration material and other information. Be creative and reach out to people you know in the community. Talk to non-profits in the area. They are masterful at finding ways to make volunteering work. The rewards to your students are countless including exposure to lots of other kinds of people, what it means to give for nothing in return, and another opportunity to work collaboratively.

Modeling and Consistency of Coherent Structures

In the next chapter, staff support structures around the benefits of instructional coherence will emphasize the need for college readiness techniques to be used across all subject areas. Some of these include note taking, how to learn from feedback (on tests, papers, and other assessments), and effective collaborative group work. Everyone reading this has experienced school-wide commitments to instructional strategies, dress code rules and procedures, tardy policies, etc. And nearly everyone has experience with what happens when a small percentage of the staff chooses to *not* implement them consistently. The most impressive and effective schools have teachers who are willing and able to have conversations with their peers who make these choices. Equally notable are schools where *students* ask their teachers why a coherent structure exists in all classes except that one.

Successful Early College High Schools extend coherent structures to the instructional realm. There is no exact list of the structures needed for success both in high school and college, but with your colleagues, you should be able to produce a list of those that, in your collective experiences, are most important. For example, the authors feel strongly that students need both rubrics and models or exemplars to be successful. These visual cues lend to transparency of the expectations as well as clarify confusion. Remember - well over half of your students are more successful with visual cues.

Let's look more closely at a potential example for your school. Most ECHS staff agree that students struggle with note-taking. Modeling the structure is one of the proactive measures to take, as well as displaying the exemplar or anchor chart permanently in the classrooms. Additionally, college instructors would welcome this knowledge and while they might not participate the same way, it is likely that they're willing to spend 2 – 3 classes purposefully cueing the students when something is important to write down. Furthermore, this open dialogue with your college partners affirms the partnership as you work side-by-side work to help students.

Like with anything, go to the world wide web for ideas! A Google search of "YouTube Cornell Notes," resulted in pages of hits. While many adults do not think of YouTube for education, today's students definitely do.

This model shown was found on Google Images, generously labeled for reuse. It is an excellent example to share with the students.

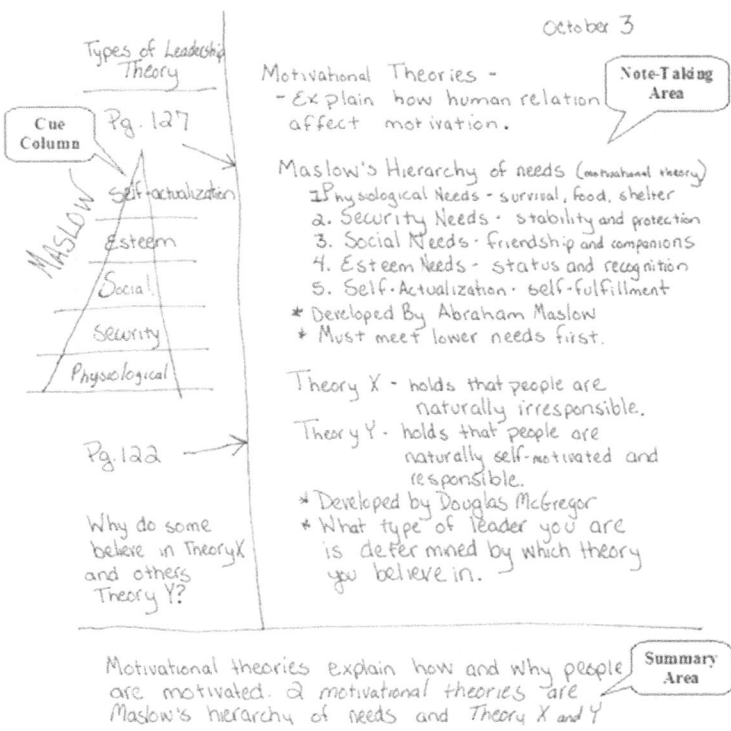

Source: http://jomzup.tumblr.com/post/74725675913

Imagine the value of posting an example like this as an anchor chart or model for students to easily reference.

During your college readiness class, go over exemplars of notes with all students. Step through the thought process and how each student should aspire to take notes like this. Additionally, outline the requirements for notes in all classes, including college classes. This will need to be monitored. Initially ECHS teachers should check the notes but do not make the mistake of simply making a requirement. Like any rule, it is much more powerful to explain *why* students need to do the notes.

Work with your staff to identify other coherent structures that need to be in place for all students to be successful <u>and how to model them for success</u>.

EXAMPLE OF THREE COHERENT STRUCTURES AGREED UPON BY AN ECHS STAFF

Instructional Strategy	Specific component agreed upon by all teachers
COLLABORATIVE GROUP WORK (CGW)	DEFINED COMPONENT: Agree on roles that will be used in all classes so that students truly gain proficiency in those areas *while in different settings*. Roles might include **summarizer**, **vocabulary master**, and **connector**. SET UP FOR STUDENTS: Teachers can create a skit during summer bridge 'over-acting' each role that they think is important. COHERENT STRUCTURE: All teachers use those three roles once each week in September and agree to debrief at October PLC meeting.
WRITING TO LEARN (WTL)	DEFINED COMPONENT: Low stakes writing that allows students to clarify thinking is a 'best practice' in all schools. SET UP: ECHS teachers can agree to all model a 'good' response so that students have clarity around expectations. COHERENT STRUCTURE: all teachers use Writing to Learn twice per class meeting.
CLASSROOM TALK (CT)	DEFINED COMPONENT: Opportunities for students to have structured academic conversations. SET UP: Again, the teachers can model during summer bridge or at the beginning of school. COHERENT STRUCTURE: All teachers give students three vocabulary words that should be spoken during the CT protocol.

It is worth mentioning that in addition to modeling academic structures, the ECHS staff must lead the acceleration of mature interpersonal behavior among students. Only through purposeful conversation by the principal and teachers will this happen. This applies to both student-teacher/instructor conversations as well as peer-peer conversations. Tell them that negative peer pressure is not acceptable. For example, in middle school, many students learned that it was not 'cool' to be smart. At your Early College, it IS cool to be smart and everyone can be successful. And the students do not know this – they need you to tell them.

And all of these components work when 1 - you are clear to the student as to *why* they are doing this process; and 2 - the adults on staff commit 100% to the agreed upon structure. It is very, very easy to introduce Cornell Notes in summer bridge or during the first week of school and assume that the students will continue to use the process without ever mentioning it again. It simply won't happen that way. It is deliberate, hard work that makes the ECHS instructional structures work.

Note: while it is not research-based, our experience with many schools and principals and students has convinced us that the use of the Common Instructional Framework by all teachers in a school results in students possessing the habits of mind necessary for college success. Some include communication, collaboration, and self responsibility.

Summer Bridge

Most Early Colleges work with their IHE partner to develop a 3-5 day summer camp or summer bridge to help prepare students for the new high school and college that they are entering. The curriculum typically focuses on the systems of the school and college, as well as a quick preparation for the college entrance exam that most entering freshmen take. While it may seem futile for underprepared students to take the college entrance exam, it provides a baseline measure for focused work. Many of the tests provide feedback to help develop a focused remediation plan. ECHS classroom teachers like to have the data as well.

Because summer bridge programs vary widely, instead we offer a list of questions that you and your college partner will want to answer in order to best frame the program to support student needs?

1. What is the budget? From the school district? From the IHE?

2. How many days? What timeframe each day? This answer is directly related to the budget.

3. Where will the summer bridge be held? For ECHSs not on the college campus, it is a good idea to hold portions of the summer bridge on the IHE campus.

4. Who will staff the summer bridge? School district teachers? IHE instructors? IHE advisors? Liaison? Are their salaries included in the budget? Or is this part of the full-year contract?

5. What supplies are needed? Who will provide them?

6. What meals are offered? Who will provide them?

7. How will students be transported from their homes for summer bridge? Between campuses (if applicable)?

8. What curriculum will be used? How can you best focus on critical reading, writing, and mathematics in order to help prepare for the college entrance exam?

9. Is there a way to differentiate the curriculum based on need? For example, will students who have already earned credit for Algebra 1 be grouped with students who have not yet taken that course?

10. What team building activities are planned? What is the focus of these activities (some ECHSs have students from one or

two feeder middle schools and students already know one another while large districts have many feeder schools and need to be purposeful in building healthy adolescent relationships with each other).

TEN QUICK AND EASY TEAM BUILDING ACTIVITIES

http://tinyurl.com/jg4bdzs

AN EPIC LIST OF TEAM BUILDING ACTIVITIES

http://tinyurl.com/zfw5g8n

TEAM BUILDING

TEAM BUILDING ACTIVITIES

http://tinyurl.com/hcwogkk

FREE TEAM BUILDING ACTIVITIES

http://tinyurl.com/hk48rna

11. When will students take the college entrance exam? Will they take all parts during summer bridge or just portions? If not all, when will that occur?

12. Will there be pre- and post-testing to determine the effectiveness of the summer bridge curriculum? Will the pre-test help drive instruction during summer bridge?

13. Is summer bridge only for freshmen? What other groups might you serve? Is it possible to have juniors on campus during the same week to serve as mentors to the new cohort? What costs will that include? What structures would need to be put into place for the juniors to be successful mentors?

14. Will the freshmen tour the campus? Who will conduct the tour? How will you keep them focused on the important aspects? What are the group sizes?

15. What part of the curriculum focuses on habits of mind? On note taking skills? On communication skills? On mature behavior, especially when in the college classes? On expectations?

16. If you have netbooks, laptops, or other devices to issue to the students, will you do so at summer bridge? At the beginning so they can use them during that camp? What preparation needs to be done by your school district tech team? The IHE tech team (for wifi and students accounts)? Will you take them back up until school starts? How will you keep track of their usernames and passwords (and you really do want to help with that!).

17. Who will help transition between activities, campuses, meals, etc.?

18. Will there be an information or education session for parents? A session where parents and their children are together? In Spanish where there is a significant Spanish-speaking population?

19. Will the students meet their college instructors? Will they see a college class?

20. Will the students learn about the syllabus and other systems used in college classes (like Blackboard or other software platforms)?

21. How will students connect with their ECHS teachers? Are there opportunities to be in small groups so the relationship can begin to develop?

The summer bridge will be a new experience for your students. ECHSs are so very good at making students feel important and convincing them that they will succeed. These intangible outcomes will make an incredible difference. As a staff, spend time discussing this paragraph, share ideas that have worked previously, and discuss the importance of rigor and relationships.

Tracey K. Hurst and Patricia E. Uribe

Chapter 4 - Staff Support Structures

This chapter complements chapter 3 in that many of the topics could easily and understandably appear as student support structures. The intent of the previous chapter was to really focus on the pieces where the student is the center of the structure. The following structures predominately involve the work of the adults on campus, in preparation for their time with students. For example, pacing guides and syllabi, addressed in this chapter, are developed and utilized by the teachers and curriculum departments, and of course, used by the student to help set them up for success around time management.

Instructional Coherence

Principals - DO NOT SKIP THIS SECTION

It is arguably the most important instructional component of successful schools and while it is more conceptual than coaching or rounds, it encompasses the work. It is the goal you should be striving to reach.

According to Newmann, Smith, Allensworth and Byrk (2001), instructional program coherence is, "...a set of interrelated programs for students and staff that are guided by a common framework for curriculum, instruction, assessment, and learning climate and are pursued over a sustained period." Additionally, they identify three conditions that will prevail when instructional coherence is strong.

- A common instructional framework to guide curriculum, teaching and assessment which leads to a climate of learning
- Staff working conditions support implementation of the common instructional framework including professional development and accountability around the framework
- The school successfully uses its resources to maintain a stable curriculum, assessment system, and teaching responsibilities over time.

"When children see themselves developing competence, they are more motivated to work, because fulfilling the basic human need for mastery builds confidence that exerting effort will bring success" (Amex & Amex, 1990).

Early College High Schools across the country, through the work of Jobs for the Future (JFF) and their state agencies, use a Common Instructional Framework (CIF) that is comprised of six instructional strategies:

Writing To Learn (WTL) Typically an individual activity, low stakes writing is designed to help both students and teachers check for understanding as well as clarify perceptions and level of understanding.

Classroom Talk (CT) The complement to WTL, Classroom Talk is also low stakes but in paired conversations. This collaborative approach provides opportunities whereby partners and triads can clarify misunderstandings and share perspectives.

Collaborative Group Work (CGW) The purposeful grouping of students in 2s, 3s, or more to collectively complete a task that otherwise would prove difficult if attempted alone. This work must be well planned with high level questions to be answered and complex tasked to be completed.

Literacy Groups (LG) - They are a form of Collaborative Group Work where students analyze the text of a content area. This might be literature in ELA or a high level trigonometry problem in mathematics. It typically uses roles to help scaffold the process for the group.

Questioning (Q) - Included in all good frameworks, questioning is the use of purposefully, planned questions that push thinking and are designed to communicate true understanding of a concept. Typically these are higher level questions that do not have short 1-2 word answers.

Scaffolding (S) - The processes used to support learning and include rubrics, anticipatory sets and other systemic protocols to help students focus on mastery of objectives.

The strategies collectively result in classrooms that are student-centered and focus on learning. With a commitment from the full staff and led by the principal, all classroom instruction is classified to fit into this framework. For example, Cornell Notes, already adopted by many schools, encompass Scaffolding, Writing to Learn and Questioning without any teacher modification to the protocol. Instead, the teachers view Cornell Notes a, "Writing to Learn," activity because it does incorporate the description above, allowing students to clarify their thinking and organize the information.

The teacher using the CIF can identify how any part of the lesson fits into the framework, or how it doesn't. The continued emphasis with the teachers that this is simply a framework that creates the conditions necessary for instructional coherence - it is not one more thing, it is a framework for instruction at this school - and it IS good for student learning.

In the previous years, ECHSs in Texas, North Carolina, and other states that worked with the national organization, *Jobs for the Future,* partnered with state education agencies, have had training around this framework, identifying instructional techniques that are effective for differentiation as well as acceleration (being ready for full time college as a high school junior). This training focused on instructional coherence in the big picture, and helped individual teachers see how the Common Instructional Framework looks in their respective classes. For example, in a workshop setting, math teachers experience the effectiveness of Writing to Learn in their content area. Previously lecture-centered teachers learn to employ Classroom Talk strategies to provide clarity of understanding, and all teachers learn how to effectively use Collaborative Groups. Most importantly, when at ECHS regional meetings and workshop, the benefit of sitting with other ECHS teachers who do the same job provides assurances that the model works.

Schools need to continually invest in professional development and the growth mindset because complacency can truly defeat years of gains. Consider this realistic scenario: a new English teacher (experienced but new to the ECHS) is using what he believes is a Collaborative Group Work activity by having students 1 - take turns reading passages in groups of four (instead of the way he used to call on one student at a time to read in the full class setting) and then 2 - answering low-level questions from those passages. The principal or coach needs to help the teacher better understand that CGW is simply not the geographic clustering of desks to do *the same tasks* previously done in the full classroom setting, and that CT (Classroom Talk) activities need to engage the students with purpose.

Now, by asking the teacher to explain how the activity fits in to the framework, a coach or experienced practitioner of the Common Instructional Framework might help him realize that the cognitive demands on the students have not changed from the old methodology. Additional coaching would help him see that by planning higher level questions (for example, instead of *What does Holden think of in his flashback after dancing with the women?* to frame the question for deeper discussion: *How does the dancing stir memories for Holden? Have you ever had one event make you remember another event?* This will likely deepen learning for students when they make these connections.) Thus, the framework is part of the common language of the campus - a key to attaining instructional coherence, and the realization of improved instructional technique by the English teacher is accelerated by use of an instructional coach or principal.

While the changes are subtle, this example conveys the content he thinks is important while providing an impetus to get students to understand that literary flashbacks are like their own memories - they make connections - which is a form of **scaffolding**. Also, students will be more engaged because they can offer their own experiences while talking about Holden's, and students feel more successful. Despite the enthusiastic teacher's love of J.D. Salinger's work, he must remember that his students most likely do not share that level of affection.

At your next PLC meeting, have teachers reflect on their practice from their previous lessons. Ask the question: *What did you do in a small group setting that could not be achieved in a full-class setting?* By posing the question, you will help them compare and the two and think critically about the importance of the very need for a difference. You can ask for responses, or instead, have teachers pair up and pose this question (where the host teacher fills in the blank):

HOST TEACHER: *If you were a student in my class and I had you in a small group doing ____, would you understand that I wanted you to learn ____?*

RESPONDING TEACHER should give a professional, objective response. Coach the teachers that if they think they want to make a suggestion or recommendation, they use the time-tested starter, *I wonder if...*

EXAMPLE 1:

SPEAKING TEACHER : *If you were a student in my class and I had you in a small group <u>identifying vocabulary words that are challenging</u>, would you understand that I wanted you to learn <u>that you should highlight or list challenging words when you read independently?</u>*

RESPONDING TEACHER: *I think that because I am a college-educated adult, I would know that. But based on my experiences in my own classroom, I've learned that explicit directions and follow-up activities will reinforce the activity. So I've had them do something like that for homework.*

EXAMPLE 2:

SPEAKING TEACHER: : *If you were a student in my class and I had you in a small group <u>rounding numbers to the nearest thousandth,</u> would you understand that I wanted you to learn <u>that skill to use on any future example?</u>*

RESPONDING TEACHER: *I would know that problems like that are probably on the homework, but I might not worry if I don't fully understand because I can copy someone else's answers. I wonder if you give each student in the group different problems, then have them rotate and check the answers if that would help.*

Including 5-10 minute activities like this where collegial conversations occur during PLC time reinforces the philosophy that we are all life long learners, and as hard as it is <u>for all adults</u> to hear that there might be a better way or that they might not be doing something correctly, it does *not mean that they are bad teachers.* It means that they are open to new ideas and absolutely focused on student learning.

For many teachers, transitioning away from traditional or 'stand and deliver' methods is a challenge, but again attainable by using the Common Instructional Framework (CIF). The key to success – the principal leading the transition. But rather than focusing on what not to do, lead the entire staff (yes, counselors and other support staff included) on what TO DO. Typically, you will have professionals that will embrace the CIF; some that already do parts of it and will appreciate the value of the structure; some that will dabble in it; and others that will resist. As the leader, you make it non-negotiable. A school's primary function is student learning; the use of a common instructional framework to achieve instructional coherence is a proven means to improve student performance (Newmann, F., Smith, B., Allensworth, E., & Bryk, A. 2001).

Also, it is easy to allow excuses to dominate PLCs (Professional Learning Communities) and informal conversations. **Don't allow it**. Principals should not allow it; and teachers should not allow colleagues to focus on excuses. Like any program adopted by schools, when followed to fidelity with leaders monitoring the program daily and all stakeholders well educated in their roles, the Common Instructional Framework has resulted in Early College High Schools markedly outperforming their other district schools as well as comparison groups of students.

Block Scheduling

If you are following the college schedule, you have to purposefully transition teachers. Moving to an 80-90 minute class period two or three times each week rather than 50-60 minutes daily is a challenge and needs attention. Teachers often struggle to effectively use their time. As consultants, we almost always find 50% or more of teachers on a campus who simply slow their pace and cover the 60-minute lesson in the allocated 80-90 minute block. This is most obvious in skills-based classrooms where it is difficult to move forward until skill mastery is achieved. For example, Algebra 1 students progress through a unit of study, continuously tackling more difficult problems.

Algebra 1 Unit Plan

	Traditional (4 x 55 min) 220 min Algebra 1	Block (2 x 90 min) 180 min Algebra 1
Monday	Review - factors; introduce factoring perfect squares; practice; preview simple trinomial factoring	Review factors; introduce factoring perfect squares and simple trinomials where $a = 1$. Practice.
Tuesday	Review homework; review factoring perfect squares; introduce trinomial factoring where $a=1$	
Wednesday	Review homework; review perfect squares and basic trinomial factoring; intentionally discuss factor pairs; introduce more complex problems where $a \geq 2$.	Review homework; clarify; move to more difficult problems where $a \geq 2$; word problems
Thursday	Look at word problems that are solved by factoring trinomials that are set up by students; practice setting up the trinomial based on the words	

The above example is reality and the problem your teachers will have (especially your math teachers who will *do the math*) is that they think the students cannot progress through as quickly and definitely not in the reduced time allocated in a block schedule. They can - it is just that the approach must be thought out differently and proper scaffolding incorporated. One idea that has become popular with both teachers and students is the flipped classroom. The basics are covered in a video that is watched by students *before* a lesson, and then the practice is done during class so that the teacher can help when needed. Teachers on block schedules particularly like this because they feel like instructional time is recovered.

As the building principal, your job is to support this *new* look - whether flipped classroom or another idea – and keep teachers from falling into the trap of doing, "... what we've always done;" to ask *why* the sequence has to be such; and help teachers use the data to better help the students. For example, the graphic on the previous page shows challenging math content. Thus including some easier, even unrelated topics for 20 minutes of the block (known as spiraling content and skills) is better than just giving the student an opportunity to do homework. For example, determine the best use of that 20-minute block by analyzing unit test data from earlier in the semester. Or talk to the students' science teacher and determine areas where students' application skills are weak. The time spent with the math teacher must be considered valuable by the students and the teacher. It is typically a difficult course for the target population and frankly, valuing the instructional time must be a priority when planning.

Professional development on this transition, clustering and scaffolding, will truly help staff improve. This is where the use of the Common Instructional Framework (CIF) is so very important. By purposefully adding collaborative group work, scaffolds, writing to learn opportunities, and classroom talk to the week-long plan below, the students will accomplish the same student expectations in just over 80% of the time allocated in the traditional schedule.

Teachers will need professional support if you want instruction time to be maximized. It may be training from an outside source or someone in your district, or taking time to visit another campus to talk to teachers who have become proficient in this area. The World Wide Web is full of opportunities to learn from formal professional development videos to informal blogs about what works. Search the topic you're teaching followed by, "lesson plan," and hundreds of hits with detailed ideas emerge. Working to effectively and efficiently use the block schedule must be purposeful and without excuses.

Don't make the mistake of assuming because a campus has used block scheduling, that it will necessarily serve as a model - so many schools waste instructional time, and in our experience, too little time has been spent examining how to avoid this. More importantly, systems need to be put into place for you to monitor the change. **There is nothing more powerful than an instructional leader in the role of principal**.

Pacing Guides

One of the simplest starting points is a basic pacing guide completed even before the syllabus, and including all of the Student Expectations (SEs) or Student Learning Outcomes (SLOs) typically put into units of study. Below is an example of a World History pacing guide that simply provides topics and time frames.

Sample Pacing Guide

	Cycle 1	Cycle 2	Cycle 3	Cycle 4	Cycle 5	Cycle 6
WEEK 1	Chapter 1 THE RISE OF THE FIRST CIVILIZATIONS	Chapter 7 ABBASID DECLINE AND THE SPREAD OF ISLAMIC CIVILIZATION:Indian Ocean	Chapter 11 THE AMERICAS ON THE EVE OF INVASION	Chapter 20 AFRICA AND THE AFRICANS IN THE AGE OF THE ATLANTIC SLAVE TRADE	Chapter 26 CIVILIZATIONS IN CRISIS: THE OTTOMAN EMPIRE, ISLAMIC HEARTLANDS AND QING CHINA	Chapter 34 AFRICA, THE MIDDLE EAST, AND ASIA IN THE ERA OF INDEPENDENCE
WEEK 2	Chapter 2 CLASSICAL CIVILIZATION: CHINA	Chapter 8 AFRICAN CIVILIZATIONS AND THE SPREAD OF ISLAM	Chapter 15 THE WEST AND THE CHANGING WORLD BALANCE	Chapter 21 THE MUSLIM EMPIRES	Chapter 27 RUSSIA AND JAPAN: INDUSTRIALIZATION OUTSIDE THE WEST	AP EXAM/ TAKS REVIEW WEEK
WEEK 3	Chapter 3 CLASSICAL CIVILIZATION: INDIA	Chapter 9/10 CIVILIZATION IN EASTERN and western Europe	Chapter 16 THE TRANSFORMATION OF THE WEST, 1450-1750	Chapter 22 ASIAN TRANSITIONS IN AN AGE OF GLOBAL CHANGE	Chapter 28/29 WORLD WAR I - THE WORLD IN THE 1920S	chapter 35 REBIRTH AND REVOLUTION: NATION BUILDING IN EAST ASIA
WEEK 4	Chapter 4 CLASSICAL CIVILIZATION IN THE MEDITERRANEAN: GREECE AND ROME	Chapter 12 REUNIFICATION AND RENAISSANCE IN CHINA: THE TANG AND SONG DYNASTIES	Chapter 17 THE WEST AND THE WORLD, 1450-1750	Chapter 23 THE EMERGENCE OF INDUSTRIAL SOCIETY IN THE WEST: 1750-1914	Chapter 29/30 THE WORLD IN THE 1920S – DEPRESSION AND AUTHORITARIAN RESPONSE	REVIEW WEEK
WEEK 5	Chapter 5 THE CLASSICAL PERIOD: DIRECTIONS, DIVERSITIES, AND DECLINES	Chapter 13 THE SPREAD OF CHINESE CIVILIZATION: JAPAN, KOREA, AND VIETNAM	Chapter 18 THE RISE OF RUSSIA	Chapter 24 INDUSTRIALISM AND IMPERIALISM: MAKING THE EUROPEAN GLOBAL ORDER	Chapter 31/32 WORLD WAR II – EAST AND WEST DURING THE ERA OF THE COLD WAR	AP US History Intro
WEEK 6	Chapter 6 THE FIRST GLOBAL CIVILIZATION: THE RISE AND SPREAD OF ISLAM	Chapter 14 THE LAST GREAT NOMADIC CHALLENGES: FROM CHINNGIS KHAN TO TIMUR	Chapter 19 EARLY LATIN AMERICA	Chapter 25 THE CONSOLIDATION OF LATIN AMERICA 1830-1920	Chapter 33 LATIN AMERICA: REVOLUTION AND REACTION IN THE 20TH CENTURY	AP US History Intro

The pacing guide is the personal scope and sequence for that classroom teacher, and is customized to fit into your school district's calendar, state standardized tests, AP exams, etc. It is a transparent communication of what will be taught and when. It benefits teachers, students, parents, and administrators.

When you require this, teachers might argue that the school district or teacher's edition of the textbook has this information. That is absolutely true BUT once the teachers are forced to put it in a calendar format like this, the teacher gains a large degree of ownership.

PACING GUIDES – BENEFITS

STAKEHOLDER	BENEFITS
Teacher	Identify *how* to "fit it all in." Often teachers struggle with this, and when and unexpected snow day or hurricane week off of school occurs, it helps identify areas where original plans will need adjustment. The World History Pacing Guide example was a product of teachers struggling to fit the large amount of content into approximately 140 days of instruction. The results on the AP exam went up significantly in the district in large part because all of the material was covered.
Principal/ Administrator	Identify if the class is on pace to compete the required SEs by the state test, AP exam, etc. Also, during walk-throughs, evaluators can quickly check that the content being learned is on pace.
Students/ Parents	Expectations are clear and there is a beginning understanding on the use of a syllabus in a course. If the teacher includes major texts and quizzes, this helps students and parents plan (see ex 2).
Colleagues	Instructional coherence includes an integrated approach to curriculum. By sharing your pacing guide with colleagues, they will know what each other is covering and when it is being covered. It allows other content areas to reinforce information. This is an incredible benefit to students as they work to make connections to the material.

Returning to the pacing guide example, you'll notice the last two weeks are dedicated to the next course. This 'solution' is offered for a couple of reasons. The *perception* of what a future teacher is (and isn't) takes little time to permeate the grapevine among students *and* parents. Because of the small school setting, shifting teachers to now instruct their future cohort is really quite easy. Make it a low-stakes setting - no tests, but the best of what the teacher has to offer. Require use of CGW and college-level readings for that next course create scaffolding lessons to truly get the students interested in the required summer reading; create SAT/ACT stations that use the test format but with information that they should know for that class; anything that challenges the students with the 'real person' at the front of the room. So, the use of the last two weeks of the year to both 1- regain instructional time (albeit for the next school year) and 2- get to know the teacher in a low-stakes, *Oh my gosh; she is a real human being,* setting is priceless. Whatever you choose to do during this time - make it meaningful. It is truly unacceptable to do any less.

Syllabus Development and Use

While the pacing guide will communicate the class scope & sequence, the syllabus will provide a comprehensive view of the course, and more importantly, expose the students to the format used in most colleges. Again, systemic use of the syllabus will maximize its benefits. Too often, the teachers distribute the syllabus and never reference it again. ECHS teachers have to teach the students how to use the syllabus, when to refer to it, and how it can guide students on the topics to study for examinations. They should regularly refer to it - perhaps at the beginning of each unit of study or every Friday to preview the upcoming week. You might be thinking that this is a student support structure – absolutely. But also think of how it helps the teacher stay focused and truly provide a rigorous course that bridges concepts previously learned to those that will be explored in college.

Initially, principals should give teachers parameters to follow when developing syllabi, much like colleges and universities do, but allow teachers to create on their own. This is an excellent opportunity to partner with your college. As the principal, work with your liaison and college deans. Have your Algebra 2 teacher ask the College Algebra teacher for her syllabus and specifically what is required by the college. Not only is valuable information shared, this low-stakes, non-subjective setting, is a great place to begin to forge a professional relationship. Furthermore, utilizing the same format will simulate the college experience, exposing students to a common practice with the individuality of their instructors. Some parameters might include course description, materials needed for class, policies (ex: attendance, participation, cell phone use), ethical expectations, office or tutoring hours and assessments. A good overview of such parameters can be found at http://tinyurl.com/zv7pven.

The high school instructors might scaffold the process by including the terminology found in a college syllabus but not necessarily topics needed their high school course. The list might include office hours (rather than tutoring), prerequisites (give students familiarity with this concept), and credits earned to name a few.

Example as it might appear on syllabus:

Mrs. Teacher

Course: Algebra 2 (1 credit)

Prerequisites: Algebra 1; Geometry recommended

Office Hours: M, W, F   8:00 - 8:45

While these might not be viewed as necessary, they do provide an opportunity to open discussion between the high school instructor and students. It is far more preferable for a 14-year-old student to ask questions about the new word *prerequisites,* the acronym listed on the required text - *ISBN,* or ask what *digitial dropboxes* are in the safer environment of a freshmen algebra class than to ask in a larger lecture setting at the college. Furthermore, the 14-year old is *less likely or unlikely* to even ask the question because he or she is significantly younger than his classmates whose ages potentially range from ages 19 - 49.

Creating systems whereby the syllabi are used by both teachers and students must be a deliberate practice. For example, if students are required to have a copy of each syllabus readily available, require the teachers to post them online on the school's web site. This practice has other obvious benefits including communication to parents and modeling for other professionals and schools.

Instructional Coaching

Typically, convincing you of the value of instructional coaching by citing research is where we like to start. The problem is that identifying reliable research which credits the addition of one isolated variable - instructional coaching - as the factor for improvement is not readily available. Research groups have difficulty, if not find it impossible, to isolate that variable in such a way that it can be measured. For example, the many facets that comprise a the instructional components of a school change even between two school years in the same building:

- the knowledge of the individual teachers
- the knowledge base of support staff
- the experience of the leader
- the class schedule that is used

Despite the research limitations, we are confident that instructional coaching is a key factor to ECHS success. Let's look at why you want to include an instructional coaching program in your professional development plan and how it accelerates the transition to instructional coherence.

Consider posting this in your teacher lounge as a friendly reminder.

All skill development benefits from coaching.

Teaching is a skill.

Bill Gates has a coach to help him gain proficiency in the game of bridge. Most Hollywood actors have a coach for their craft. There are business coaches, skills coaches, performance coaches, and newly popular life coaches. Tutors are coaches. Teachers are coaches. Anything worth developing a skill around has a coach. Yet, some educators are reluctant to embrace the idea of an instructional coach (IC), so it is important that you make a sound decision in your selection of an IC; support that candidate's professional development into the role; and work deliberately to keep that role working to fidelity and deny the urge to let the administrative demands bleed into it.

Effective coaches have a combination of skills, and like any profession, strengths will vary. You want a person that is **mature**, maintains a **professional demeanor,** and **connects well with people** - all people. This is your starting point but that last point is arguably the most important. Remember, the coach is charged with being a part of your leadership team *without the power to enforce anything at all.* True, the coach can 'report' back to the principal, but that will not sit well with the teachers (and understandably so). It is truly a delicate balance – one where the coach must have the trust of the principal....and of the teachers.

As your understanding of the value and possibilities for your IC develops, more factors will be added to your list. For example, it is more important that the IC is adept at **asking conceptual or 'big**

picture' questions than that he/she can converse in all content areas. Your coach needs to be a **problem-solver** because there is no 'one-size-fits-all' solution.

Below is a list of coaching questions - you can assess a teacher's readiness to coach if he or she can develop these kinds of questions and skillfully use them with a teacher in a coaching session.

<u>Good Coaching Questions – example: coaching a teacher to improve Writing to Learn (WTL) strategies:</u>

1. How will the low stakes writing activity communicate to you that the students have mastered the objective?

2. What is it about the WTL that allows the teacher to know that mastery was attained by individual students? What is it about the activity that is a marker to indicate success, mediocrity, incompleteness, failure? How do you help the students master this self-evaluation process?

3. Are you confident that low-stakes writing is the best way to check for understanding in this situation? Is there a scaffolding Classroom Talk activity that might help students clarify thinking before trying to put their ideas in their own words?

4. How do you model great answers? Since students want to do well, is there a way that they can view a 'model' response when they finish? I wonder if you have ever seen a teacher posting A-B-C response models where student work representing the grades *A, B,* and *C* are displayed, so the students can do a quick gallery walk to better understand and self-evaluate.

While you were reading, were you thinking of someone you know that can question like this?

Now ask yourself,

1.   Is that person **mature** enough to serve in this role, maintaining a level of trust with the staff and with me?

2.   Does that person maintain a **professional demeanor** in every aspect of the job? Does he/she dress professionally, speak respectfully to adults and children, have a philosophy of continuous self-improvement? Does he share my philosophy because if he doesn't, I need to stop thinking of him as a candidate now.

3.   How does that person **connect with other staff members**? If I asked the rest of the staff to use 2 or 3 words to describe the IC candidate, what would they say? Is the candidate perceived as sincere, honest, and trustworthy?

Some might argue that an important fourth question would be, "Is the person trusted by his/her peers?" Trust is earned and while the individual might be trusted as a peer (example - trusted as a teacher), when the teacher transitions into the role of coach, trust in that position must be developed. Some issues that might be faced include resentment by two or three others because they were not chosen; confusion around the role of the coach; or perception that the job is easy. Clear communication about your choice can help some with this situation.

While there is a level of experience that is necessary in order to speak the language of learning, your instructional coach does not have to be the most experienced teacher on your staff. Consider the questions below.

What characteristics will you look for in the instructional coach?

1. Does the candidate provide a good model of instruction every day in his/her classroom? (It is difficult for the rest of the staff to follow someone who is at times lazy, doesn't plan lessons, fails to provide rigorous lessons, and all of the other instructional demands you expect from them.) Does the candidate follow the norms and expectations of the principal? (It is equally difficult to follow someone who thinks the rules don't apply to them - arrives late, leaves early, doesn't turn in required lesson plans, let's students leave early for lunch, doesn't teach bell to bell, etc.)?

2. How much experience does the candidate have in training adults? What kind of evaluations did he/she get from the participants?

3. How good is the candidate's understanding of learning theory? Most likely the candidate was a good teacher - how well will he/she transfer this practice to other subjects when coaching?

4. Is the candidate well-versed and experienced at lesson planning and understands planning with the end in mind?

5. What leadership experience does the candidate have? Was he/she involved in committee work? Department chair? Curriculum writing? These are important to assess the ability to work with peers. What leadership qualities emerged during your tenure on campus?

6. Is the candidate well organized, never misses deadlines, prompt and concerned about time management?

7. Can he/she listen and effectively act on concerns? Is the candidate empathetic to the concerns of staff?

8. Does he/she understand the strengths and weaknesses of co-workers? Additionally, does the person possess the skill to determine the motivations for their work in order to help guide them? Think of this example: when coaching a sport, an athletic coach learns that some players work hard for the coach; some for the love of the game; some are avid rule followers; some are pleasers - this is true of all groups.

Making Connections

When developing your coaching program, look at what we do know. Jim Knight, a well respected leader in instructional coaching, cites that in his doctoral research, "...teachers were four times more likely to implement teaching practices they learned during partnership sessions than those they learned in traditional sessions (Knight, 2007)." This shouldn't surprise you because these teachers were able to **make connections** that applied to their classroom, situation, or school needs. Their learning was scaffolded by the instructional coach. They saw the value of what was stated by a peer - someone they know - in a small group setting, whether it is an internal instructional coach (one of them) or external coach (employed specifically to help them on this journey).

Personal connections make learning real! Affecting another person can really hit home. Consider the following:

Paula, new to your school, but a 7-year veteran of teaching, needs to learn about the Common Instructional Framework and rounds. She is the only new teacher for the school year, and you are committed to providing her with the support she needs to understand the work that is done at your ECHS. Which scenario will most likely prepare her to acclimate to your school?

Scenario 1: Attend a state-wide conference on the Common Instructional Framework and rounds

Scenario 2: Watch supporting videos on the Common Instructional Framework as well as go the Regional Service Center and attend a 6 hour session on rounds

Scenario 3: Work with your instructional coach for 3 hours on the day she signs her contract, going over written information on the CIF and rounds, as well as looking at parts of the video that the Regional Service Center uses. The IC and Paula agree to meet again (at least a week later) where Paula can ask questions; your IC can clarify points and give some examples of work from the previous year. (Then during the summer bridge camp, Paula sees the Framework in action while one of the veteran teachers uses it with incoming freshmen.)

Of course Scenario 3 is the best choice. So often professional development is given in large doses in the summer and full implementation, weeks later, is the expectation. The reality is that we need to take in the new ideas in pieces, try it out, talk about what worked and what didn't, problem solve, and build on our own successes, as well as the successes of colleagues.

People are the same everywhere - young or old. They want to have a purpose or reason. Thus your instructional coach must be adept at making connections: making connections with people; helping teachers connect what they are doing to the bigger concepts; connecting teachers in like contents and across contents.

While we detailed the importance of connections with those scenarios, there are other qualities to consider. The importance of **maturity** and **professionalism** are perhaps more obvious. You want your IC to serve as a role model, both inside and outside of your building. You want someone that focuses on learning and not on the distractions. You need someone that you can trust. When the IC delivers professional development to the entire staff, it must be a serious, goal driven event, much like an effective class. The instructional framework must be employed providing a model of the strategies in action *with* purposeful debrief <u>connecting</u> it to their respective classrooms.

<u>How will you define the role of the instructional coach?</u>

1. What do you want the instructional coach (IC) to do?

2. How will you differentiate an IC from a mentor?

3. What percent of an FTE do you have for the instructional coach?

4. What financial resources do you have to pay the instructional coach? Do you have funds to pay for 15-20 extra days in the contract (many schools pay for 5 days after the traditional contract and 10 before)

5. How will you select the instructional coach?

6. How will you communicate your selection to the staff?

7. How will you define the role with the IC? How will you define the role with your staff?

8. How will you keep yourself from turning this person into a quasi-administrator?

9. How will *you* coach that IC to grow in that position? If you don't have the ability or time, who can fill that need?

10. Can this IC work side by side with another teacher without the teacher viewing the coach as a threat?

One of the biggest issues you will face after finding the perfect instructional coach is sustaining the position. Typically, professionals chosen for IC are later chosen to move onward and upward. Some become administrators; some pursue their doctorate. Some simply move away.

So ask yourself these questions:

1.   Do I expect my IC to stay at my school for three or more years? Is it worth the training investment so I see the return with my teachers?   (That is how a for-profit business would think but it doesn't mean it is the right answer; it *is* something you need to think about.)

2.   If I think the IC will leave, what else can I do to sustain the work?

3.   Is my IC able to balance the demands of the job with the teaching load? How have I adjusted the master schedule to allow my IC time to coach - when is the release period(s)? Will outside trainings be a burden? Have I talked to him/her about necessary travel for trainings?

4.   Is my IC highly organized?

5.   Is there a way to apply a succession plan without creating insecurities?

6.   Will the role of my IC in Year 1 be the same as in Year 3? Year 5?

Some schools split the IC job between two teachers.   The rationale is sound – often the best teachers are selected to be the coach and by making that change, the best teachers are no longer working with students. By using two coaches part time, they both are still working directly with children. Additionally, having them both serve as models for the teacher cadre is powerful. Imagine the end of a professional development session on collaborative group work where both coaches encourage teachers to visit their classrooms to see the theories in action.

Even after visiting or talking with nearly every ECHS that was among the first 62 designated in Texas, we've never seen the exact instructional coaching model employed twice. We share this because it is important to know there *is not a perfect model*. There is your perfect model that is continually reexamined, checked, adjusted and responds to the needs of your campus. Work through the questions to develop a job description; share that with your selected coach and the staff – clarity and transparency are of the utmost importance when building a successful program; revisit the role each spring or summer to confirm that it is best for student learning on your campus.

Instructional Rounds

Inviting other professionals to your school to examine the good work you are doing is healthy. It is done by successful organizations from Fortune 500 Companies to small non-profit organizations. For example, Curt Carlson, President & CEO of SRI International, has a ventures group come from outside of his company and spend part of a day with his group to critique the innovations they are working on and to make ideas better (C-Span2, 2013).

In education, instructional rounds are a widely accepted tool for improvement. As the practice gains popularity across the country, scholars like Robert Marzano and Elizabeth City are among the most widely respected on the topic. Marzano states, "Instructional rounds are one of the most valuable tools that a school or district can use to enhance teachers' pedagogical skills and develop a culture of collaboration" (Marzano, 2011). Elizabeth City, co-author of the popular Harvard publication, Instructional Rounds, helps explain the purpose with, "Rounds are not about 'fixing' individual teachers. Rounds are about understanding what's happening in the classrooms, how we as a system produce those effects, and how we can move closer to producing the learning we want to see" (City, 2011).

In Early College High Schools, instructional rounds serve as a tool to shift teachers toward a culture of learning - not only for students but for professionals. Rounds provides an opportunity for professionals to collect data in the classroom - data that can truly help teachers improve student learning.

The typical progression of the Harvard model of instructional rounds includes the school staff identifying theory(ies) of action and corresponding problem(s) of practice; visits by professionals from outside the campus to collect data and identify trends; and analysis and actions taken by the staff in response to the visit. If considering engaging in the Harvard model of rounds, the following steps can guide you:

1. **Read Instructional Rounds by Elizabeth City, et al, 2009, or better yet, have a book study with your staff.** This may seem like a time consuming endeavor, but you and your teachers will have the same conceptual understanding, and the conversations you have during PLC time will provide everyone with clarity, enrich understanding, and create buy in.

2. **Conduct a professional development session with your teachers whereby you correlate the 7 principles outlined in the book with your mission, vision and belief statements.** You can do this if you feel well educated and experienced at the process. If you are concerned about your own expertise or committing the necessary time, contact your outside facilitator for the event and see if he/she can Skype in to host a Q&A during your meeting. As the leader, know that it is important that you believe these principles. Also, while your entire staff may not be totally on board, you need to plan to lead them on this mission.

3. **Facilitate a meeting with all or parts of your staff whereby a Theory of Action (or multiple theories) based on the instructional core are discussed.** From that, a Problem of Practice is defined and becomes the focus of the upcoming visit.

4. **Set up the visit!**

a. Invite professionals from your district and region. You will want at least five groups of 3 - 5 people so that a broad view of the school is possible. They will need to commit to the entire work session (typically 5 hours with a working lunch that you provide).

b. **Find an outside facilitator** who can remain objective. This should be someone well versed in rounds, and ideally, not connected directly to your campus.

c. **Reserve a room** where the rounds visitors can fit comfortably, working in teams no larger than five. *Your staff should not participate in classroom visits.*

d. **Develop a schedule** to visit as many classrooms as possible, with each group staying in a room for 18-20 minutes. The longer one group stays in a particular classroom, the broader the view from which to collect data. Also, schedule groups so they see a variety of content areas.

e. **Develop a data collection sheet that lists your Theory of Action (ToA) and Problem of Practice (PoP), as well as guiding questions to help participants**. These questions should be directly related to the POP and scaffold the process for the participant. It is best to have a separate data collection sheet for each room visited, so in the example above, each group would have five data collection sheets.

f. **Shopping list** for the host: sticky notes in a variety of colors (each group uses a different color); chart paper; markers; scotch tape; highlighters; pens, clip boards.

Sample Rounds Schedule

TEACHER/	SUBJECT	9:00 - 9:15	9:15 - 9:30	9:30 - 9:45	9:50 - 10:05	10:10 - 10:25	10:30 - 10:45
SMITH 124	PRE-AP ENGLISH I			Group 3	Group 5		Group 10
RAMIREZ 142	PRE-AP ENGLISH II	Study Tour Overview with Tracey		Group 4	Group 6	Group 8	Group 9
SILVER 102	CREATIVE WRITING			Group 5	Group 7	Group 9	Group 3
JOHNSON 121	ENGLISH 3			Group 6	Group 8	Group 10	Group 4
BELLOW 133	AP STATISTICS	It is important to go over the structure and purpose of the study tour.		Group 7	Group 9	Group 6	Group 5
MONTRIVO 124	PRE-AP GEOMETRY			Group 8	Group 10	Group 4	Group 7
BARGER 111	STAAR MATH (ALG I - DB)		But here she has veteran rounds participants get started because they know about the structures. She still values their day (in this case principals) by offering them small group time while the rest of the group rounds the classes.	Group 9	Group 3	Group 3	Group 6
MOREALES 142	AQR			Group 10	Group 4	Group 5	Group 8
ALISON 140	JOURNALISM			Group 1	Group 2		
DELAHOME 138	AP WORLD HISTORY			Group 2	Group 1	Group 7	
ENDICOTT 139	PRE AP BIOLOGY	Group 1	Group 2				
SMITH 144	PRE AP PHYSICS	Group 2	Group 1	Principals (Groups 1 & 2) meet with Tracey			

Try to keep time in classrooms to about two hours. It should be enough time for visitors to see a variety and visit every teachers' class.

5. Typical 'day of' schedule

8:15 – 8:30 Check in and Group Assignments (provide juice, coffee, and donuts)

8:30 – 9:25 Welcome and Overview of Day; Make visitors familiar with

- *Problem of Practice*
- *Observing: Learning to See, Unlearning to Judge*
- *Schedule of Observations*

9:25 – 12:00   Classroom Observations

12:30 – 2:00   Working Lunch

Observation Debrief: Description, Analysis, Prediction

- *In small groups*

2:00 – 2:45 The Next Level of Work: Recommendations and Reflections

- *Whole Group Debrief*

6. Next steps

- *How the school uses the data*
- *Subsequent rounds events*

While the Harvard model of rounds is widely accepted and practiced in early college high schools, the logistics are sometimes a challenge.   Having outside visitors spend 5 hours on campus, providing them with lunch, making and following the visitation schedule, all after having developed a sound problem of practice with the staff, is often taken on by the principal - the sole administrator on many ECHS campuses.   (It is worth reminding everyone that the ECHS principal still completes all the tasks a traditional high school principal faces with regards to student learning - attendance, grades, district policies, state policies, etc. - work typically done by a staff of 4 or 5 administrators in a traditional high school.) AND, while the time the 'invited' professionals dedicate to a campus that is not their own provides information on the rounds process, and is of course benevolent, it simply cannot occur very frequently due to their own job responsibilities.

With that in mind, many ECHSs who embrace the process may have one or two of these previously described rounds visits in a school year, but many interpreted the work of by Robert Marzano (2011) and focused on engaging professionals on campus in a form of rounds that has the school staff visiting one another on a more regular basis. The school still identifies areas where work needs to be examined, but individual teachers create observation questions for visitors.

At Pinnacle ECHS in Athens, Texas, founding principal, Jami Ivey, worked with her staff and developed a schedule whereby teachers would identify the school's needs as it related to the school's goal of active engagement. During a pre-rounds session, the host teacher clearly articulates the data that they want collected; he is observed; and then he gets feedback from colleagues that afternoon or the next morning - again, all in a controlled protocol system.

By examining the schedule on the next page, you see that Allen was rounded on 11-6-12. He developed questions for his colleagues around literacy groups, a form of collaborative group work, and use of the iPad. Warning - developing questions is a skill. As you can imagine, the quality of the question(s) can change the value of the process. You will want to help the staff with this. The questions should afford the observers the opportunity to truly collect data, thought not necessarily in the sense that it will be strictly number collection, but it will be something that is objective. For example, the third question on the example provided on the next page, "Are the students using the iPad effectively?" would be a typical question used in rounds but as you can see, without context, can mean different things to different observers. Thus, during pre-rounds, the host teacher can give context.

PINNACLE ROUNDS SCHEDULE

Date	Teacher	Strategy
9/11/2011	Tilley	
9/18/2011	Aleman	1. Write to Learn
9/25/2011	Allen	2. Cornell Note Taking
10/2/2011	Feeler	3. iPad
10/9/2011	Sikes	
10/16/2011	Deas	
10/23/2011	Tilley	
10/30/2011	Aleman	
11/6/2011	Allen	1. Collaborative Group Work
11/13/2011	Feeler	2. Ipad
11/20/2011	Thanksgiving Break	
11/27/2011	Sikes	
12/4/2011	Deas	

Here are some samples of questions that this social studies teacher might ask his colleagues to examine:

Sample Learning Question	Context given by teacher during prerounds
1. Are the student roles in the literacy groups resulting in equal participation by all four members?	*The roles are Group Leader, Connector, Text Evidence Collector, and Illustrator. They are analyzing three primary source documents, and ranking them according to the importance based on the individual group's focus.*
2. Are the groups working collectively to rank the documents or is their evidence that they dividing up the work?	*One of the biggest challenges of group work is to avoid the 'divide and conquer' mentality that has been accepted by other teachers - so the students think it is okay.*
3. Are the students using the IPAD effectively?	*To me, 'effectively' means that they are using it to fulfill the task and/or deepen their understanding of the day's objectives.*

How can you make this work for your ECHS? Optimally, you will lead this. Realistically, that requires you, the leader, to delegate other duties so you can focus on this important instructional component. Be cognizant that you must communicate to the staff that it is *your* desire to have instructional rounds occur on campus, and that you are making it a priority in all of your work days.

Question: Does the principal participate in this form of rounds?

It is up to the principal. Remaining objective is the key, and the benefit of participating is that you are exemplifying your role as the instructional leader by being there with the team visiting classes. The drawback is that when evaluatory concerns occur during the rounds visit, it is impossible to 'forget' them during the formal evaluation process, even if it is clustered in a general statement. Some principals use 'feed forward' techniques whereby they ask leading questions to help the host teacher decide how to use the information from the rounds session.

Question: How often should a teacher be 'rounded' or visited?

At least once each semester, and as often as once a month. The latter might seem excessive, but as the process becomes commonplace, it will become a part of the day. You will know that your school has truly embraced this concept of transparency when students do not even turn their heads when the classroom door opens. They will grow accustom to the 'learning' that their teachers are modeling.

Question: Do counselors and other support staff need to participate?

Suggestion: YES!!! You are all in this together. Anyone that is charged with student learning and growth can offer valuable insight. Their perspectives can accelerate the movement toward instructional coherence and exemplary teaching.

Question: How do we avoid hurt feelings?

Suggestion: Use a facilitator - it can be someone on staff whose job is to redirect any subjective statement back to the speaker and ask for it to be reworded as an objective statement. That alone will minimize the problem. Through a bit of practice, the facilitator masters the art of requiring participants to use objective statements. An expert facilitator will even take an objective statement like, "Students were texting and not working," and suggest the observing teacher quantify the statement. The result is something like, , " 5 students were texting when you were giving directions," provides objective observations. The host teacher is astute enough to draw the conclusion that those students were not working.

Looking At Student Work (LASW)

Teachers look at their own students' work every day: sometimes in a low stakes setting where no grade is attached; other times in the realm of quizzes, essays, tests, etc. That is not the purpose of this section.

Looking At Student Work (LASW) is a formal attempt to examine teaching and learning based on the products of the learner. While Instructional Rounds looks at the process, this purposeful work looks at the product with the idea that in the end, the student learning outcomes must be demonstrated, especially in this high stakes testing environment. This section will introduce you to the concept, tell you why it is important in the work of the ECHS, and provide guidance for a deeper study. There are great resources that can deepen your learning on the topic.

Many different protocols are widely accepted, and they serve specific purposes. As a leader, it is not recommended that you dictate one protocol - instead, when implementing LASW as part of the imbedded professional development, choose 3 or 4 protocols that truly serve different purposes. Then let the host teacher determine which protocol works best based on his/her needs. Time estimates are included, but know that any time you introduce a new idea, practice or protocol, everyone needs some time to gain familiarity.

Other planning logistics

You will need, at minimum, one hour of time to work through a protocol. Early College High Schools have professional development time embedded in the work day; this is a great use of that time. Again, don't allow this professional development time to be used for administrative issues; the intent is to use it for professional growth around how students learn.

Host teachers will:

1 - identify a learning gap, a question about learning that they have wondered about, or perhaps even look at the work holistically

2 - work with the instructional coach or principal, identify a protocol that will complement the goal

3 - stay focused on #1 during the actual protocol

4 - reflect and make changes in instruction to impact student learning

The work of Harvard University's Project Zero recommends that the facilitator help the group to stay focused on the evidence and avoid judgments. This is no different than the work around instructional rounds. A good facilitator will always force you back to the evidence. For example, look at the scenario below. This or something like it will likely happen when you embark on the process.

Looking at Student Work Scenario

Likely Scenario

Facilitator: Let's examine the student work and look for evidence of students making inferences, as requested by our host teacher, Mr. Smith.

Ms. A: I have a piece where a student wrote, "I think the author wanted us to remember what happened in chapter 2 where Kelly saw the confrontation and it was foreshadowing for the fight in chapter 8. He wants us to remember without having to rewrite it."

Mr. B: I have something like that too. On my paper a student wrote, "When Bill and Alex fought in the beginning of the book, Kelly saw it. I inferred that Kelly still remembers it even though the author didn't write about it but wrote, 'Kelly seemed to be drifting away from the conversation.'"

Ms. C: I think that most of the students figured that out.

Facilitator: (looking at Ms. C): Do you have additional evidence on your student work? Respectfully, that is why we are here. I know it might seem like an easy inference that most students should be able to make, but we need to give Ms. Smith something like, "17 of 20," or "all but one," so that we start to see patterns and trends.

When a facilitator is meek or unwilling to redirect or even correct a peer, it reduces the impact of the work. As the instructional leader, you can facilitate this process. LASW is perceived as a 'safe' environment by teachers because the group is looking at the *students'* work rather than the teachers' instruction; during rounds, principals are discouraged from doing anything but observing the debrief because despite all efforts to focus only on student learning, there is an obvious connection to the *teacher's* work and thus it is examined to a greater degree. During LASW, it seems to be less of a conflict.

Whether as the facilitator, a participant, or an observer, the principal should absolutely be a part of the process. As the instructional leader on your campus, the serious nature of the work starts with you! Take part - no, lead this process. Look more holistically at what is happening; make connections to other parts of the learning process in your school; look for patterns; as you see/hear something that fosters a memory or idea, write it down -

you'll think of models, examples that will help staff members. And note all successes and celebrate them with your staff. Even embracing the process is a celebratory point - change is hard for all humans; lead them down that road.

Have individual conversations with teachers afterward. *What did you learn from participating? Did you think of another question we need to pursue? How might we benefit from expanding this process?* You'll find that the process will become a natural part of being a staff member at your school. It is part of the job. You'll start asking candidates for jobs: "Are you familiar with rounds and LASW? How do you feel about these processes?"

Frequently Asked Questions about ECHS Instruction

1. Do we need to use the Common Instructional Framework?

You need to use *a common instructional framework*, but not necessarily the CIF outlined here as developed by Jobs for the Future. We strongly encourage inclusion of this CIF. This work is research-based and when working with other ECHSs, this common language is a powerful tool. The components of the CIF are not unique to this framework - after all, scaffolding has always been a part of teaching - but it is the power of using the six strategies in unison that results in rigorous, college-preparatory classes.

2. Do we need to use instructional rounds?

Again, the research shows that the facilitated collegial conversations that result from an intentional rounds process is good for student learning.

3. How do we maintain the rigor of the class with such different ability levels represented?

This challenge is faced by every classroom teacher. The proper use of the Common Instructional Framework results in differentiated instruction. For example, if a teacher gives her world geography class a Writing to Learn prompt, *"What push and pull factors are in play in our town or any town where you have lived?"* the students will respond 1 - at their current writing level; and 2 - based on their own experiences. With an additional scaffolds like, "Think about jobs, housing, and schools in your answer," students will be able to write to things they know and connect to the learning and that day's lesson on migration. By adding those key words (jobs, housing, and schools), the teacher is truly tying the WTL to the daily objective.

4. **How do we help students know to self-assess their own progress and mastery?**

This is a purposeful and relentless task that must be taken on by every teacher, every day. The *release of learning*, as coined by Fisher and Frey (2009), outlines the purposeful planning steps to engage learners and give them responsibility for their learning. These four parts of any lesson - focus lesson, guided instruction, collaborative learning, and independent learning - will result in opportunities for both the teacher and the student to assess competence and mastery.

Chapter 5 - Classroom Systems

All great classrooms, regardless of the grade level, have systems in place to help the process of learning. Do you have a system when the students enter class? Do they begin solving a warm up problem that is projected or get their journal and begin writing? That is a system. When the timer buzzes indicating the next activity, do the students already know their roles during the transition? Can they perform this *low stakes, non-academic* activity flawlessly? Do they know the rationale behind these effective routines and transitions? The journal writers return the notebooks to the crate, and the problem solvers check answers with their *elbow partners*, all without being told. The sound of the timer going off is their cue. Again, these are systems. In the most effective classrooms, students know their role from the time they enter these until they leave. There is an expectation that the systems will be followed, and with few exceptions, when a teacher sets these expectations, students meet them. And each of these small tasks has been taught, reviewed, and backed up with rationale from the teacher. It is not sufficient to say, "My system is that the students know to listen to me." That results in wasted time, bored students, and missed opportunities.

Typically, teachers that complain that routines do not work have not followed through by using them regularly or have not fully developed a routine to eliminate problem areas. They expect that by telling students something once, it should be a routine. As consultants, we can attest to the fact that *adults* don't follow through with only one set of verbal directions, rules, and even subsequent routines. The point is that, like anything, if you value the routine, repeatedly support that work.

This chapter is not to serve as a resource on each of these well documented topics (lesson planning, routines, etc.), but to briefly review them and discuss their importance in being predominant in every classroom of the Early College High School and when done by all staff, the emergence of now coherent structures that will accelerate learning on your campus. Consider the fact that as an Early College High School, you are charged with preparing students for a full college credit load, 12-15 hours, for their junior year of high school. That urgency must be felt by everyone on staff, along with adherence to the design elements. It is the key to success.

Valuing Instruction Time

There are so many opportunities to lose valuable instruction time. The obvious causes include state mandated testing, district mandated benchmarks, routine annual health screenings or records updates, general school announcements, late buses, and even the college being closed (which reminds you to compare your calendars!).

But consider the lost time when a teacher doesn't have a routine for a warm up or the teacher who does have a routine, but has a weak warm up or an activity unrelated to the day's objective. What about the classroom where transitions from one activity to the next are slow and tedious? Handing back corrected assignments and quizzes can also be a time waster. Have you ever entered a classroom or even just walked by when there are five full minutes left in the class period only to see the students packed up and the teacher at her desk? These and many more comprise the hours and hours of lost instruction time in each class each school year. That five minutes at the end of the period times 180 school days is FIFTEEN hours of instruction.

Instructional time is the most valuable commodity a teacher has. Teaching bell to bell, planning learning activities where students progress toward mastery, and constant evaluation of the processes

Do you have a routine or set of rules for students when they...
...enter the room?
...transitior to and from groups?
...write in their journals or other WTL activities?
...need to sharpen their pencil or other logistics?

Think about what it takes to maximize instruction time? What can you do to make these necessary transitions quick and smooth?

and products is the job of an educator - all educators. Teachers plan and implement; principals support the process by serving as the instructional leader, providing feedback, and asking questions. The principal does not need to know all of the content to serve as the instructional leader, instead, asking questions like:

"How do you think the students were able to grasp the larger concept?"

"What systems are in place for safety in the lab activity?"

"Where do you think the two groups in the back of the room lost focus?"

"I noticed that you called on the boys in the class to answer 12 of the 14 questions you asked. Did you mean to do that?"

"Describe how you planned the transition from the collaborative group work to the independent practice."

"These are the questions that you asked, and all but one was at the basic knowledge level. Can we work together to develop higher level questions?"

Thus, the instructional leader exemplifies the value placed on instruction time by 1 - being in the classrooms A LOT (each room 2-3 times each week, even for only a minute or two); 2 - being there as the instructional leader and not necessarily as the evaluator; 3 - asking questions like those above; 4 - and most importantly, showing the teachers that you are first and foremost interested in student learning. Some principals question the value of quick trips to the classrooms. Any trip to the classroom is valuable. Patterns emerge and the principal becomes just another part of the learning process.

Once the principal models that student learning in a rigorous setting is a priority, teachers will both understand the expectations and work very hard to achieve those goals.

Lesson Planning

The most important skill that continually needs reflection is lesson planning. Much has been written on the subject, but this blog entry captures the essence of the importance:

First of all, a planned lesson is just better. Not all planned lessons are fabulous and not all unplanned lessons are a disaster, but even a bad lesson will be less bad planned, and even a great lesson can be greater with a plan. If you are good at teaching unplanned lessons, you will be even better at teaching with a plan.

(The Official Blog of Teach and Learn with Georgia, 2012) Read the rest of Georgia's blog at http://tinyurl.com/j5qll3e.

The lesson plan serves as documentation of what goes well and what doesn't. Students know when teachers have planned or not, and visitors including other teachers, school district personnel, and the principal, definitely know if the lesson was planned. Simply putting a few tasks to paper is not a plan.

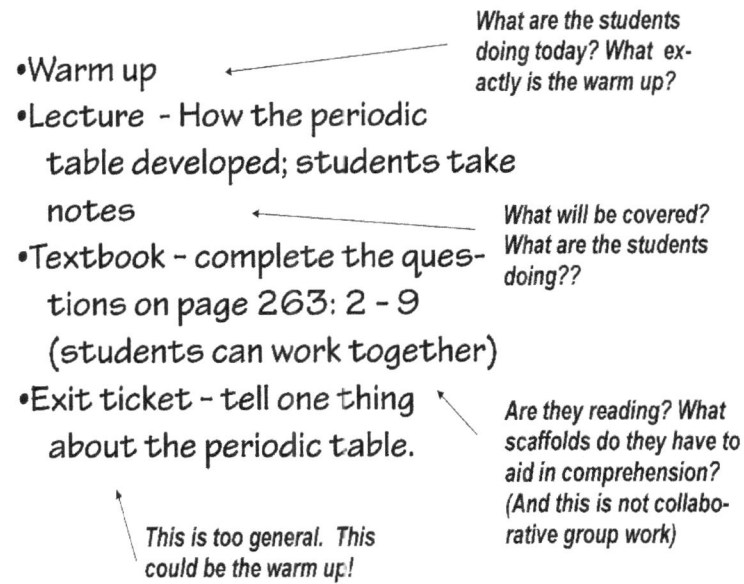

Not a lesson plan

•Warm up ← *What are the students doing today? What exactly is the warm up?*

•Lecture - How the periodic table developed; students take notes ← *What will be covered? What are the students doing??*

•Textbook – complete the questions on page 263: 2 - 9 (students can work together)

•Exit ticket – tell one thing about the periodic table. *Are they reading? What scaffolds do they have to aid in comprehension? (And this is not collaborative group work)*

This is too general. This could be the warm up!

While the above is not a lesson plan on the periodic table, a simple Google search of, "lesson plan periodic table high school," resulted in a more detailed plan that was thought out and included a student warm up activity. There are definitely more detailed plans on the world wide web, but the purpose is to move beyond the 'list' above.

Science: Chemistry
Sample Lesson Plan: Introduction to the Periodic Table of Elements
Submitted by: Kristen Demick, Chemistry Teacher, Melrose High School

Content Objectives: To learn what an element is and the factors by which they are arranged on the Periodic Table.

Class opener/Do Now: Students will have 90 seconds to write down as many "elements" as they can think of. Then, as a class, students will share their lists, and a list of elements will be formulated on the board.

Mini-lesson: Begin with visual aides; explain how elements make up objects in every day life; exist in different phases (solid [Au and Ag jewelry], liquid [Hg in thermometer], gas [He in balloon]).

Introduce the Periodic Table:

- What is an element?
  - The simplest form of matter; cannot be decomposed into simpler substances; matter
  - composed of one kind of atom, each atom has same properties; atoms all have the same atomic number
- Break down into name and atomic symbol
  - Ex: Carbon
  - Review subatomic particles from previous unit (electrons, protons, neutrons)

Source: https://www.wolframalpha.com/educators/lessonplans/Introduction_to_the_Periodic_Table_of_Elements.pdf

---

Repeated attempts by school districts to solve personnel issues by creating mandated curricula and pre-determined activities have created an alarming number of teachers who have either abandoned this important function or never used it in the first place. Providing a sound curriculum is an excellent practice by a school district; confusing lesson planning with curriculum is a mistake made too often around the country. Large school districts everywhere want the proven curricular elements masterfully instructed by stellar instructors to automatically transfer to teachers who have not developed the same skill set. It does not happen - teaching is a skill that must be developed, coached, and continually practiced in order to improve.

While this might lean toward cynical, it is indeed intended to remind you of the reality that can easily dominate a campus if this task is overlooked by you or anyone on your staff. Be sure everyone knows the difference between curriculum and instruction; between curriculum and lesson plans; between actively engaged students and compliant students. That base measure will truly help your staff grow into great facilitators of learning in the ECHS classroom.

Curriculum
kə'rikyələm/

the subjects comprising a course of study in a school or college

Instruction
in'strəkSH(ə)n/

detailed information about HOW something should be done

Lesson Plan
'les(ə)n/   plan/

A teacher's detailed description of the learning targets and what instructional methods will be used to help all students achieve them

Lesson planning must begin with the end in mind. As Grant Wiggins and Jay McTigue (1998) skillfully communicated in their on-going work which began with, Understanding by Design, it is imperative that teachers identify desired results, determine the evidence that will demonstrate learning, and determine the activities and processes by which to get there.

Another resource that we repeatedly use as consultants is the work of Nancy Fisher and Douglas Frey (2009) where they advocate for the *release of learning* to the students. In our opinions, it is the cornerstone of active engagement practices, and has an excellent lesson design incorporated within the work. Teachers who are resistant to the shift toward active engagement need a push from the principal. Remember, resistant teachers remember learning from someone at the front of the room who disseminated all they knew about a subject while the students feverishly wrote in their notebooks. So like students, teachers need modeling and practice. Stepping out of their comfort zones is not easy but is necessary. Remind them, the research is new - most documented in the last 10-15 years. Go to http://fisherandfrey.com/ for access to more about Fisher and Frey's most recent work.

Daily Objective: _____
Use the template to plan your lesson. Include the amount of time (in minutes) spent on each part.

FOCUS LESSON	COLLABORATIVE TASK
GUIDED PRACTICE	INDEPENDENT LEARNING

Developed based on the work of Frey, Nancy, and Douglas Fisher. "The Release of Learning." *Principal leadership* 9.6 (2009): 18-22.

While reading this section you may be thinking, "Of course we need lesson planning. We do lesson planning." Here is a challenge: go to the lesson plans for the next Wednesday of classes at your school.

-Do you have those plans from every teacher?

-Are the necessary components of lesson plans present in each?

-Is there evidence that the teachers planned with the end in mind?

-Are the students actively engaged in processes for learning with the teacher never lecturing for more than 8-10 minutes at a time?

-Do they identify what a student who achieves the stated objective can do and how do they articulate that? *What does mastery look like?*

-Are they planning for the students to be the center of the learning OR for the teacher to be the center of teaching?

Active engagement of meaningful content where clear expectations of what the learning looks like is the goal, and masterful lesson planning will clearly show that. As you worked through the questions, you likely found 20-35% of your teachers are doing excellent lesson plans (and they, not by coincidence are your best instructors), another 20% that did a bad job or didn't submit plans, and the rest are somewhere in between. Almost always, this correlates to the job done in the classroom.

One of the biggest problems with lesson planning is the actual repetitive thought process of exactly what success looks like. We often challenge teachers to tell us what the student who earns an A, B, or C can do related to the objective, and what sets each apart from the others earning different grades. That thought process is not common, and when we conduct the professional development on this topic, it is among the most well received workshops. While we know that the formal practice used in our workshops is not necessarily followed to fidelity on every subsequent occasion, the feedback over the course of the past few years affirms that teachers do change their thinking about the 'end' product. Try using that question the next time you visit a planning meeting on your campus.

There are many resources available on line to learn more about lesson planning. Here are a few that we like:

(VIDEO) shows a new teacher working with an instructional coach. It is very much like the kinds of conversations that occur in successful early college high schools.

http://tinyurl.com/zhjk9yy

(ARTICLE) by Grant Wiggins really offers you information to allow you to reflect on the process whether you're new to teaching or a seasoned veteran.

http://tinyurl.com/hnra96p

(WEB RESOURCE) offers a great platform for creative and critical thinking from Harvard University.

http://tinyurl.com/hmek4bt

Routines

Classroom routines are the procedures that are put in place to address common and not so common classroom events, all so that learning can continue and instruction time is maximized. Teachers should have routines for taking attendance, returning homework, having students read the feedback on papers, and even for logistical concerns like when a student forgets his pen. Each of these routines demonstrates the value placed on instructional time. It exudes, **"I only have you for 180 minutes each week and I will help you learn during that time."** And that very quote could be in the section above on lesson planning or below on rigor. It needs to be

108

part of the culture of your school, and when you truly attain that level, the students will be hushing one another and grow impatient when their time with their teacher is interrupted for any non-academic need.

Some other routines that are not so obvious truly create a culture of learning in classrooms. Maximizing instructional time is important, so much that when students enter the classroom, they should *immediately* engage in a task that is either directly related to learning or supporting an upcoming learning activity. This must be dictated by the teacher. For example, anyone that has visited an elementary school first thing in the morning sees droves of 5-10 year old carefully putting their bags and backpacks in their assigned space, often a cubby hole as opposed to a locker, and moving to their desk where they pick up a crayon, pencil, or pen, look to the board for direction, and begin working. It might be that they're simply reading a book of their choosing, or actually engaged in a writing or a math protocol. Regardless, your students did this as elementary school children and can do this for you.

In the secondary classroom, greet them at the door. If the seating chart has changed that day, have it in hand when they enter or project it on the screen -they will be able to look at it and find their seat. Or if you are using collaborative group work in the lesson, have the list of groups in hand – 99% of the time, the teacher should purposefully group students in order to set up the lesson for success. On any given day, students should know what the expectation is when they enter the room. Typically, a warm up with practice from a previous lesson or a prompt for students to write about can truly engage the adolescents and get them focused on learning.

The same can be said for dismissal. Many early college high school do not use a bell system. The teacher dismisses the students much like a college instructor would do. Even in a situation where bells are used, it is a good idea for ECHS teachers to require students to stay in class until dismissed by the teacher – it is both good practice in courtesy, and prepares the students for college classes.

Here is an example of a routine – an **anticipation guide** helps students focus using this *Writing to Learn* activity. It serves as a *Scaffold* (another part of the CIF) by allowing students to connect to the content on a personal level. A third part of the CIF is incorporated - *Questioning*. And if the teacher has the students turn and talk about their answers, *Classroom Talk* is included. The more the routine is used, the better the student products; the better the questions posed by the teacher, the deeper the ensuing conversations. As you can see, it is easy to make and can even be projected so students can write in their journals or notebooks.

ANTCIPATION GUIDE

Write all you know about helicopters:

Write one question you have about how helicopters work.

What do you know about the Smithsonian Institution?

The Air & Space Museum is just one of the museums of the Smithsonian but it is located on two sites that are 30 miles apart. That's almost as far apart as Downtown Dallas to Downtown Fort Worth. Why do you think the museum sites are this far apart?

The authors created this anticipation guide when consulting with the Smithsonian Institution, connecting them with Dallas area middle schools for an outreach program about helicopters at the National Air & Space Museum..

Routines used for academic activities will also maximize instructional time. Using Writing to Learn (WTL) protocols daily is recommended and some teachers make use of dedicated notebooks to journal them. Have a crate for each class, and students pick up (and return) their own as they enter and leave class. (An added bonus of this system is that by using it every day, you can quickly take attendance by noting those notebooks still in the crate.)

Have a set of 4-5 good Writing to Learn prompts that are numbered so that you can easily direct them to a prompt or maybe let them roll a die to determine which prompt (for rolls of 5 or 6, they can choose any of the four).

What are the two most important things that I have said in the last 10 minutes? *1*

Write out the steps on how to solve the last problem we did together. *3*

Even though you understand everything so far, what might a classmate be con-fused by and why? *2*

Look at today's objective and write what you think we have already cov-ered what we might do next. *4*

Successful use of Classroom Talk (CT) is dependent on good protocols and routines. One reason that teachers avoid CT is actually a failure to teach the students *how* to participate in an academic conversation. Making the assumption that this has already occurred is unfortunate and unrealistic. To reinforce this point, we have done many professional development sessions where we have had to put many scaffolds in place for successful academic conversations among the adults. Some of the easiest to employ require simply stating <u>and</u> posting one or two of the following:

- "Use the following three vocabulary words" (then list them)

- "Get into groups of three; A – talk; B – listen; C - write down how many times you hear A say the three vocabulary words. " (then rotate roles; use a timer)

- Use a poster to model CT starters

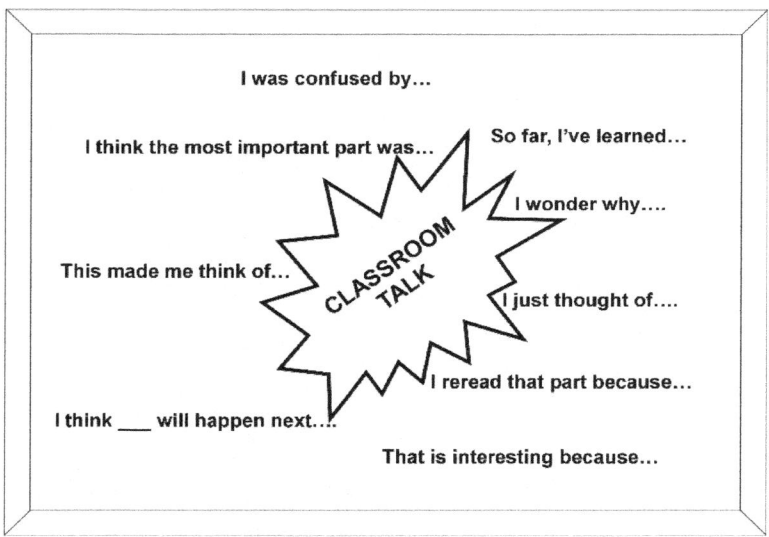

- Tell the students to talk as a historical figure would talk (or another good role model). Melody Townsell at Gilliam Collegiate in Dallas used to tell her freshmen, "Now say it like the President would say it," in order to get her students to leave adolescent slang outside of the classroom doors

- Require the students to answer in a specified number of words or syllables. Use haiku poems (where they have to count the syllables) or tell them, "Give me a 6-word definition for ONOMATOPOEIA."

Visit these websites for some excellent ideas around developing classroom routines:

 http://tinyurl.com/622ty

 http://tinyurl.com/z9ukpkj

Rigor in the Classroom

Rigor is indeed a buzz word in 21st Century learning. Many of us are familiar with, Rigor is Not a Four-Letter Word, by Barbara R. Blackburn. Much like the approach to lesson planning, ECHS faculty need to spend a couple of meaningful hours *together* planning with the end in mind regarding their agreed upon definition of an *ECHS graduate*. We have done this activity with most schools with whom we have worked: What does an ECHS graduate look like? What skills does he have? What content does he know? How does he advocate for himself? How does he interact in groups? What are his academic behaviors?

One way to do this work with your staff is to start with an individual Writing to Learn activity:

What does a _____ ECHS graduate look like?

Work independently, then with a partner, and then with your group to create a vision of what a graduate from your school can do, say, think about, etc. Use the graphic organizer below to help.

Reading	Writing/Speaking
Mathematics	Thinking
Habits of Mind	What Else?

Then using any of a number of debriefing protocols, teachers discuss their answers and come to a consensus about the areas in the boxes above and naturally come up with additional areas to include. The point is that together, there is a collective vision and then....with purposeful on-going professional development, this vision is revisited often.

In conclusion, we hope that we have addressed the many structures and systems, along with the design principles employed by successful Early College High Schools. The most difficult part in writing is finding a stopping point. As we finish these guidebooks, it is our intent to fully develop the web page, www.echsguidebook.com (where we will post the graphics from the books) and begin offering workshops at Early Colleges where we address additional information and make hard copies of these books available to participants. Thank you so much for your interest. Reach us at echsguidebook@gmail.com.

Appendix A - Acronyms

AVID - Advancement via Individual Determination

CIF - Common Instructional Framework*

* CT - Classroom Talk

* CGW - Collaborative Group Work

* LG - Literacy Groups

* WTL - Writing to Learn

ECHS - Early College High School

ELL - English Language Learner

IEP - Individual Education Plan

IHE - Institution of Higher Education

ISD - Independent School District

LPAC -Language Proficiency Assessment Committee

MOU - Memorandum of Understanding

SAC - Southern Association of Colleges

TEA - Texas Education Agency

THECB - Texas Higher Education Coordinating Board

TSI - Texas Success Initiative

*Jobs for the Future (jff.org) developed the specific CIF used in ECHSs in Texas and North Carolina, among others. Writing to Learn, Classroom Talk, etc. are well-accepted strategies that are referenced in multiple publications.

Appendix B - Links to Websites and Videos

Websites

ECHS Guidebooks   http://echsguidebook.com

Authors of this work, Tracey K. Hurst and Patricia E. Uribe, provide a web page that links to resources and information on all aspects of the ECHS design.

Association of Supervision and Curriculum Development
http://www.ascd.org/Default.aspx

The Association for Supervision and Curriculum Development, or ASCD, is a membership-based nonprofit organization. Members range from superintendents, principals, teachers, professors of education, and other educators and they rely on ASCD for professional development in the area of curriculum and instruction. Its mission is to develop programs, products, and services essential to the way educators learn, teach, and lead.

Early College Designs http://www.jff.org/initiatives/early-college-designs

http://www.earlycolleges.org/overview.html

Early College Design on the national level is often spearheaded by Jobs for the Future, a non profit organization. According to their website (www.jff.org), "Jobs for the Future works to ensure that all underprepared young people and workers have the skills and credentials needed to succeed in our economy by creating solutions that catalyze change in our education and workforce delivery systems. Working with our partners, JFF designs and drives the adoption of innovative and scalable education and career training models and systems that lead from college readiness to career advancement. We also develop and advocate for the federal and state policies needed to support these solutions."

Early College High Schools in Texas http://www.txechs.com/

This web page links you to the Texas-specific documents like the ECHS Blueprint, dual credit FAQs, and TSI information, to name a few.

Educate Texas http://www.edtx.org/

Educate Texas is an innovative public-private partnership focused on a common goal: Improving the public education system so that every Texas student is prepared for success in school, in the workforce, and in life. Educate Texas has been among the organizations leading the ECHS movement in Texas.

Kansas Coaching Project: Instructional Coaching
http://www.instructionalcoach.org/

The purpose of the Kansas Coaching Project is to study factors related to professional learning and how to improve academic outcomes for students through supports provided by instructional coaches. Instructional coaches are onsite professional developers who teach educators how to use evidence-based teaching practices and to support them in learning and applying these practices in a variety of educational settings.

Looking at Student Work
http://www.lasw.org/

http://www.essentialschools.org/resources/60

Looking at Student Work is a highly regarded process whereby educators look purposefully at the learning products. Protocols assist groups in the process.

The Teaching Channel https://www.teachingchannel.org/

The Teaching Channel's mission is to create an environment where teachers can watch, share, and learn new techniques to help every student grow. Working side by side with school districts and other education agencies, they have created an excellent repository of best practices, as well as other supporting materials.

Texas Association of Secondary School Principals
http://www.tassp.org/

TASSP's purpose is to build an active network of educators that want to take responsibility for the quality of school leadership. Through meetings, resources, and a 5000+ membership, they are the professional organization for most of Texas' public school principals and assistant principals.

Texas Education Agency http://tea.texas.gov/

Among its many responsibilities, Texas Education Agency oversees the designation of multiple public school programs, including Early College High School.

Texas Higher Education Coordinating Board
http://www.thecb.state.tx.us/

The Texas Higher Education Coordinating Board's stated mission is to promote access, affordability, quality, success, and cost efficiency in the state's institutions of higher education, through Closing the Gaps and its successor plan, resulting in a globally competent workforce that positions Texas as an international leader in an increasingly complex world economy. It is an active partner with TEA in promoting and sustaining the ECHS movement.

Appendix C - Texas Success Initiative (TSI)

"TSI Met," is a phrase with which all Texas school administrators need to have great familiarity....immediately! TSI stands for Texas Success Initiative and originates from the December 2003 Texas law which defines a student's, "...readiness to perform freshmen-level academic coursework." Amended in 2006 and again in 2012, the ruling requires all Texas **public** IHEs (2 and 4 year colleges and universities) to use this standard to allow students to enroll in credit-bearing classes.

Private IHEs set their own rules and definition for "college readiness," in order to follow the THECB code.

The TSI test is written by the College Board and consistently administered across all IHEs in Texas.

TSI ASSESSMENT cut scores approved by the Coordinating Board at the April 25, 2013 Board Meeting

Approved phase-in College Ready cut-scores
Phase 1 –Freshmen entering higher education **Fall 2013 (first class day)**
 Mathematics -350

 Reading -351

 Writing –Essay Score of 5; Essay Score of 4 and Multiple Choice of 363

Phase 2 –Freshmen entering higher education **Fall 2017 (first class day)**
 Mathematics -356

 Reading -355

 Writing -Essay Score of 5; Essay Score of 4 and Multiple Choice of 363

Final –Freshmen entering higher education **Fall 2019 (first class day)**

⦿ Mathematics -369

⦿ Reading -359

⦿ Writing -Essay Score of 5; Essay Score of 4 and Multiple Choice of 363

Approved Developmental Education cut-scores (no phase-in)

Freshmen entering higher education **Fall 2013 (first class day)**
⦿ Mathematics -336
⦿ Reading -342
⦿ Writing -350
Source: http://www.thecb.state.tx.us

It is important to understand that TSI-met is not always synonymous with "College Ready." Instead it is merely a measure of high school TEKS mastery that correlates to expected success in college coursework. For example, the TEKS covered on the TSI Math test are predominately Algebra 1 TEKS, and unlike the previous TSI assessments (pre-2013/14 school year), it cannot be used for college placement (previously, colleges used the Accuplacer Math to place students, or identify which college course a student should take). Additionally, taking the TSI Math test in the week before or after taking the STAAR Algebra 1 test will definitely increase the likelihood of reaching the qualifying score BUT as the administrator, you might consider the score that would be earned by a student taking the test the following August - how much of the conceptual understanding (needed for success in College Algebra) was retained? While it would agreeably be a better indicator, the reality is that taking the test in May is still the best option. Just provide adequate review and practice before moving into the next math class in August.

According to the College Board (2013), each of the three tests has 20-24 questions and 10-12 items on the diagnostic test. It is a computerized adaptive test where the answer to an item dictates the program's selection of the next item. It is meant to provide as precise of a score as possible. In each TSI test section, there is a point where the items are identified by the College Board (not the test taker) as "diagnostic." Once in this section, the results are no longer high enough to qualify and the program provides a report to the testing institution. This report is intended to help the test-taker prepare to retake. You need to be sure to get these reports from the test center so your teachers can use the information to help the students prepare.

Appendix D - North Carolina DAP (Diagnostic Assessment & Placement Test) information

North Carolina uses an online version of the College Board's Accuplacer as an entrance test. There are four parts: mathematics, reading, revising and editing, and an essay using the College Board's WritePlacer software. The first three portions are untimed and according to the College Board (see overview of all parts of the test at this link) have 72, 30, and 20 questions respectively. The writing portion does have a time limit of two hours. To learn more about WritePlacer, follow this link.

Like most college entrance exams, the DAP is used for placement in mathematics and English classes for traditional students. The standard for qualification to take college courses typically includes a combined score of 166 on sentence skills and reading in traditional Accuplacer scoring, and varies on math resulting in course placement. Each college can adjust and your ECHS liaison should provide this information to you.

Appendix E - Crosswalk Form

Crosswalk Tracking Sheet						
Grade Level	High School Course	HS Course #	HS Credits Earned	College Course	College Course #	College Credits Earned
8th grade						
9th grade						
10th grade						
11th grade						
12th grade						

Appendix F – Bibliography

American Institute Research and SRI International. August, 2009. "Six Years and Counting: The ECHSI Matures. Fifth Annual Early College High School Initiative Evaluation Synthesis Report ."
Available at
http://www.air.org/files/ECHSI_Eval_Report_2009_081309.pdf.

Amex & Amex, 1984; Blauner, 1964; Kaufer, 1990. page 301

Augenblick, Palaich and Associates, Inc. July 2006. Denver, Colorado. RETURN ON INVESTMENT IN EARLY COLLEGE HIGH SCHOOLS.

Backstrom, R. J., 2004. Examining teacher's experiences in a small middle college. PhD. Dissertation, The University of Iowa, United States – Iowa. ProQuest Digital Dissertations database. (Publications No. AAT 3129275).

Balfanz, Robert and Nettie Legters. 2004. Locating the Dropout Crisis— Which High Schools Produce the Nation's Dropouts? Where Are They Located? Who Attends Them? Baltimore: Johns Hopkins University

Berger, Andrea et al. 2014. Early College, Continued Success: Early College High School Initiative Impact Study. Washington, DC: American Institutes for Research.

City, Elizabeth. Learning From Instructional Rounds. Education Leadership. October 2011 | Volume 69 | Number 2. page 36.

Clotfelter, C. T., Ladd, H. F., & Vigdor, J. L. (2007b, October). Teacher credentials and student achievement in high school: A cross-subject analysis with student fixed effects. Working Paper 11. Washington, DC: Urban Institute, National Center for Analysis of Longitudinal Data in Education Research. Retrieved January 25, 2008, from http://www.caldercenter.org/PDF/1001104_Teacher_Credentials_High School.pdf

College Board web site.
http://counselorworkshops.collegeboard.org/registration/southwester n-schedule. February 2015.

Conley, David. 2010. College and Career Ready: Helping All Students Succeed Beyond High School . San Francisco, CA: Jossey-Bass.

Conley, David T. March 2007. Toward a More Comprehesive Conception of College Readiness. Eugene, OR; Educational Policy Improvement Center.

C-Span2; April 17, 2013. Revolutionaries in Conversation with John Markoff, NY Times. Computer History Museum, Mountainview, CA.

Ellerson, Noelle. 2010. American Association of School Administrators. School Budgets 101.

Frey, Nancy, and Douglas Fisher. "The Release of Learning." Principal leadership 9.6 (2009): 18-22.

Garet, Michael, and Mengli Song. 2013. "Early college, early success: Early College High School Initiative impact study."

Jobs for the Future. 2014. Early College Design. http://www.jff.org/initiatives/early-college-designs.

Johnson, J., & Rochkind, J. 2010. Can I Get a Little Advice Here? How an Overstretched High School Guidance System Is Undermining Students' College Aspirations. Public Agenda.

Johnson, J., Gupta, J., Hagelskamp, C., & Hess, J. 2013. Ready, Willing, and Able? Kansas City Parents Talk About How to Improve Schools and What They Can Do to Help. Kansas City Parents Talk About How to Improve Schools and What They Can Do to Help (April 2013).

Knight, Jim. Winter. 2007. "5 Keys Points to Building a Coaching Program." NSDC, Vol 28, No 1, p 27

Lieberman, Janet E. "The early college high school concept: Requisites for success." Retrieved May 28 (2004): 2008.

Linnenbrink, E. A. & Pintrich, P.R. 2003. "The role of self-efficacy beliefs in student engagement and learning in the classroom." Reading and Writing Quarterly, 19. 119-137.

Marzano, R.J., and Waters, T., and McNulty, B.A. 2003. School leadership that works: From research to practice. Alexandria, VA: Association for Supervision and Curriculum Development.

Marzano, Robert. The Art and Science of Teaching: Making the Most of Instructional Rounds. Education Leadership. February 2011 | Volume 68 | Number 5 . Pages 80-82

McDonald, Denise and Tina Farrell. Out of the Mouths of Babes: Early College High School Students' Transformational Learning Experiences. 2012. Journal of Advanced Academics, 23(3) 217–248.

McRobbie, Joan. West Ed Policy Brief: Are Small Schools Better?. October 2001. http://www.wested.org/online_pubs/po-01-03.pdf

Newmann, F., Smith, B., Allensworth, E., & Bryk, A. (2001a). Instructional program coherence: What it is and why it should guide school improvement policy. EducationalEvaluation and Policy Analysis, 23(4), 297–321.

Nodine, Thad. 2009. Making the Grade. Boston: Jobs for the Future.

North Carolina New Schools. 2014. Changing the Future through Early College High Schools.

Rich, Lawrence Michael. 2011. A DIFFERENT TYPE OF LEADER: Characteristics of Effective Middle College and Early College Principals. Diss. University of Connecticut.

Texas Education Agency. Memorandum of Understanding - Guidance for Early College High Schools.2011. http://www.txechs.com/downloads/26_echs_-_memorandum_of_understanding.pdf

Texas Education Agency. 2013. http://www.txechs.com/what_is_echs.php.

Wasley, P.A., & Lear, R.J., March 2001. Small Schools, Real Gains. Educational Leadership, 5 (6), 22–27.

Webb, Michael and Carol Gerwin. 2014. Early College Expansion: Propelling Students to Post Secondary Success at a School Near You. Jobs for the Future. Boston, MA.

Tracey K. Hurst and Patricia E. Uribe

Tracey K. Hurst and Patricia E. Uribe

Made in the USA
Middletown, DE
26 September 2021

49116007R00086